"Olin Boles is the real de⟨ and observed as he presented th⟨ ⟩eral occasions. He has used this material in mentoring pastors and new believers. I encourage *you* to read *Second-Mile Leadership* and become a Second-Mile Leader."

Dr. Mike Smith
Director, Minister/Church Relations Department
Southern Baptist of Texas Convention

"Brother Olin lives what he writes. In our days of working together in Brazil, he spent many nights swinging in a hammock in a 100+ degree room, drove dangerous roads well after midnight, preached by candlelight, ate 'black' rice—which became white after waving off the flies—survived at times on bananas and coconut water, witnessed to folks others avoided, crossed rough bays in overloaded canoes with water lapping over the side, and flew with me over uninhabited areas for hours. What you read springs from a ministry and life impelled by love for our Lord and a deep desire to excel in knowing the joy of godly leadership."

Dr. Orman Gwynn
International Mission Board
Retired Missionary to Brazil

"Go and make disciples …" Olin Boles has taken this command seriously. He is a practicing disciple and has been making disciples for many years. He has done much to encourage and help me and many others in our journey as disciples of the Lord Jesus Christ. We are all better as a result of knowing Olin and learning these principles. These biblical principles come from his life and insights. They are practical and simple, and yet profound."

Donald Hintze
Executive Director, Gulf Coast Baptist Association
Angleton, Texas

SECOND-MILE
LEADERSHIP PRINCIPLES

Olin D. Boles

Olin Boles
Isa 40:31

CROSSBOOKS
PUBLISHING

CrossBooks™
A Division of LifeWay
1663 Liberty Drive
Bloomington, IN 47403
www.crossbooks.com
Phone: 1-866-879-0502

First published by CrossBooks 01/13/2011

ISBN: 978-1-6150-7716-8 (sc)
ISBN: 978-1-6150-7717-5 (hc)

Library of Congress Control Number: 2011920379

Printed in the United States of America

This book is printed on acid-free paper.

To my wife, Marilyn, who is a genuine second-miler in every aspect as a wife, mother, grandmother, and genuine disciple of Jesus Christ.

Contents

Foreword

Second-Mile Leadership

Every once in a while, a book comes along that grabs you by the lapels of your coat and shakes you into consciousness. Olin Boles's book, *Second-Mile Leadership*, is such a book. In a day when many Christian leaders seem content with doing only the minimum, *Second-Mile Leadership* issues a clarion call to go the extra mile. Packed with biblical principles which inspire, inform, challenge, and motivate, *Second-Mile Leadership* provides a clear road map to those who wish to pursue the high calling of spiritual leadership.

A seasoned second-mile leader himself, Olin Boles writes from a rich background of Christian ministry. Having served as a pastor, missionary, and denominational leader, he is uniquely qualified to address the challenges that confront contemporary church leaders. Both pastors and lay leaders will discover helpful insights to guide them in their quest for excellence in kingdom service. You will be immeasurably blessed as you carefully consider and conscientiously apply the principles contained in this volume.

Thank you, Olin Boles, for your creative presentation of the principles of second-mile leadership, and thank you for reminding us that second-mile leaders go the extra mile, "not because they are required by law but are compelled by love." I pray your book will be widely read.

Foreword by Dr. John A. Hatch, Executive Director, Gregg Baptist Association, Longview, Texas

Introduction

"If someone forces you to go a mile, go with him two miles" (Matthew 5:41, NIV). In the Sermon on the Mount, Jesus challenges His followers to go beyond the mile the law required and to go the extra mile compelled by love.

It is my conviction that second-mile leadership is desperately needed for these challenging days of the twenty-first century. Every Christian should strive to be known as a "second-miler."

Over the last few years, while serving as a Director of Missions of the Gulf Coast Baptist Association in Texas, I have developed what I have called Twenty-first Century Second-mile Leadership Principles. These principles have been shared with pastors, state and national leaders, and missionaries around the world, and they have been well received and used in various ways.

It is not my purpose to address leadership *methods* in this book. Rather, I will address leadership *principles*. Methods are many, principles are few, and while methods often change, principles never do.

A principle is a universal truth that is a foundation to other truths. A principle is international, inter-cultural, inter-generational, and timeless.

The purpose of these principles is twofold: to *encourage* and to *challenge* each believer in Jesus Christ to be a second-miler in every area of life. The first mile is required by law; the second mile is compelled by love. Doing only what is required will not make anyone an effective leader. Second-milers are the history-makers. The challenge for second-milers is greater now than ever before.

Becoming a twenty-first-century second-mile spiritual leader depends upon the personal spiritual transformation of each individual. As a disciple of Christ, you are committed to Him. Going the second mile should be the natural thing to do. This kind of transformation provides the determination to be all that God desires that you be. Emotional motivation is brief in duration. Spiritual transformation endures for a lifetime.

The Second-Mile Principle: In the Sermon on the Mount, Jesus says, "If anyone forces you to go one mile, go with him two miles" (Matthew 5:41, NIV).

- The mile requirement that Jesus mentions was a Roman practice that dated back to the conquering Persians six centuries earlier. The Romans had the authority to compel the Jews to bear their burdens for one mile. This practice was hated by the Jews. Outside many Jewish homes, there was a stake. One mile from their house was another stake. The Jews carried the burden the required distance and then threw it down with disgust. In this passage, Jesus is talking about how to live a joyful, satisfied life. In other words, he is talking about *attitude*. He is saying that you must do more than is required. You must be willing to go the second mile. The first mile is required by law; the second mile is compelled by love.

- Doing only what is required can be done with a minimum of motive and will not make you an effective leader. Second-milers are the history makers. The challenge for Second-milers is greater now than ever before.

- According to Wikipedia, October 14, 2005, marks the date of the dedication of the Extra Mile Points of Light Volunteer Pathway National Monument installed in the sidewalks of Washington, D.C. Markers form a one-mile walking path through an area bounded by Pennsylvania Avenue, Fifteenth Street, G Street, and Eleventh Street NW. The honorees of the monument are people who, "through their caring and personal sacrifice, reached out to others, building their dreams into movements that helped people across America and throughout the world." Each honoree has a custom-made bronze medallion installed along the path, which currently boasts twenty such medallions, but there are plans to extend the monument down to Eleventh Street and back up to F Street so it forms a mile-long pathway of seventy medallions. While your name may never appear on Extra Mile Avenue in Washington, D.C., it is my hope that one day we may hear the Lord say, "Well done, good and faithful servant; you have indeed gone the second mile."

- My challenge to you is that you will determine to be a second-mile leader in every area of your life.

Scripture: "A curse on him who is lax in doing the Lord's work!" (Jeremiah 48:10, NIV).

Prayer: Lord, help me to be a second-mile leader who is totally committed to You in all that I may attempt to be and to do. Amen.

Section One
The Call of a Second-Mile Leader

The Plow Principle: "Jesus replied, 'No one who puts his hand to the plow and looks back is fit for service in the kingdom of God'" (Luke 9:62, NIV).

- The Call: "It was he who gave some to be apostles, some to be prophets, some to be evangelists, and some to be pastors and teachers to prepare God's people for works of service so that the body of Christ might be built up" (Ephesians 4:11–12, NIV).

- The Caller: "God Himself communicates a distinctly personal summons that can only be heard by the called, but he hears it like the thunder and generally for a lifetime."[1]

- "A call means being used to impact a part of God's world, that noble and eternal part. At the same time, a call means I work where He sends me." [2]

- The Plow Principle means that you have answered God's call and have put your hands to the plow and have determined not to look back. Your eyes are fixed on Jesus, the author and finisher of your faith. When you come to the end of the row and He says the day is done, then—and then only—will you call it a day.

- There are times when only the call of God upon your life and the grace of God in your life will keep you where the will of God has placed you.

- The call of God and the engineering of our circumstances is of God, never on the ground of our usefulness. The call relates us to the purpose of God. [3]

- I remember very vividly the night that, as a seventeen-year-old, I knelt by my bedside asking God to show me very plainly whether it was His call upon my life to be a minister of the gospel, or if there was another reason for the restlessness in my spirit. His answer was plain as I prayerfully opened my Bible and found His assurance in Psalm 105:1: "O give thanks unto the Lord; call upon His name: make known his deeds among the people." This was in the spring of 1954, and for the past fifty-six years, His peace has been with me as I have had the glorious privilege of making known His deeds around the world.

Scripture: "The one who calls you is faithful and he will do it." (I Thessalonians 5:24, NIV)

Prayer: Lord, help me to always be reminded of your faithfulness and my frailness. Amen.

The Holy Ground Principle: " 'Don't come any closer,' God said. 'Take off your sandals, for the place where you are standing is holy ground.' " (Exodus 3:5, NIV)

- Second-mile leaders consider their call as something that occurred on holy ground. With the confirmation of God's call upon their lives, most can remember when and where it was that God spoke to them with inescapable assurance.

- "Being yoked with God in a holy cause makes every pastor a mighty vessel for righteousness in every setting."[4]

- "It is a great deal better to live a holy life than to talk about it. Lighthouses do not ring bells and fire cannons to call attention to their shining; they just shine." D.L. Moody

- "The proud man counts his newspaper clippings; the humble man his blessings." Bishop Fulton J. Sheen

- "Do not consider yourself to have any spiritual progress, unless you account yourself the least of all men. God walks with the humble; he reveals himself to the lowly; he gives understanding to the little ones; he discloses his meaning to the pure minds, but hides his grace from the curious and the proud." (Thomas A. Kempis)

- "We may be quite sure of three things. First, that whatever our Lord commands us, He really means us to do. Secondly, that whatever He commands is for our good always. And thirdly, that whatever He commands He is able and willing to enable us to do, *for all of God's biddings are enablings.* If God's bidding is His enabling, then our part is to discover His provision for a walk in obedience to His will, His ways and His Word." (Frances Ridley Havergal)

- "One does not choose the ministry! A pastor is chosen. He is chosen by God for God's purposes, in God's time and place, and serves Him in God's way. God has chosen to change others and our world through pastors who are called by God, who answer this call, and who obey God consistently. God has chosen to bring His people and the pastor to fullness of life. He does this by expressing Himself, His presence and power in the pastor and through the Scriptures."[5]

- "Preeminently the Lord looks for one whose heart is loyal to Him (2 Chronicles 16:9). This is a man after God's own heart! Character precedes assignment, determines assignment, and maintains assignment."[6]

Scripture: "May God himself, the God who makes everything holy and whole, make you holy and whole, put you together spirit, soul and body, and keep you fit for the coming of our Master, Jesus Christ. The One who called you is completely dependable. If he said it, he'll do it!" (I Thessalonians 5:23–24, *The Message*)

Prayer: Lord, may I always keep in mind that your call was issued on holy ground and that each place of ministry or leadership is holy ground. May I be found faithful. Amen.

The Hearing God's Voice Principle: "The watchman opens the gate for him, and the sheep listen to his voice. He calls his own sheep by name and leads them out. When he has brought out all his own, he goes on ahead of them, and his sheep follow him because they know his voice" (John 10:3–4, NIV).

- Second-mile leaders know the importance of *hearing God's voice* as they seek to give leadership to others as well as listening to what He has to say to them personally. There must be great care in being assured that they are acting according to what God has said, rather than listening to other voices that will give them misleading direction.

- For those who are sincerely seeking to be in and do God's will, the most pressing questions are these: How does one know God's voice? How can one know whether the thoughts are God's or from the devil?"

- "There are four ways in which He reveals His will to us; through the Scriptures, through providential circumstances, through the convictions of our own higher judgment, and through the inward impressions of the Holy Spirit on our minds. Where these four harmonize, it is safe to say that God speaks. For I lay it down as a foundation principle, which no one can gainsay, that of course His voice will always be in harmony with itself, no matter in how many different ways He may speak. The voices may be many, the message can be but one. If God tells me in one voice to do or to leave undone anything, He cannot possibly tell me the opposite in another voice. If there is a contradiction in the voices, the speakers cannot be the same. Therefore, my rule for distinguishing the voice of God would be to bring it to the test of this harmony."[7]

- "God doesn't use the same methods on everyone. He knows exactly what it takes in your life to get your attention; a restless spirit, a word from others, blessings, unanswered prayer, or unusual circumstances. He may use one today, and then He will employ a different one three weeks from now, something else months away, or an entirely different strategy two years from now".[8]

- Second-mile leaders keep their hearts and minds open to hear God's voice and are able to perceive that it is indeed God who has spoken.

Scripture: "The Lord came and stood there, calling as at other times 'Samuel! Samuel!' Then Samuel said, 'Speak for your servant is listening'" (NIV, I Samuel 2:10).

Prayer: Lord, my prayer is that I may always have a heart and mind that is listening for your voice. Amen

The "Hearing God's Voice through His Word" Principle: "The Lord continued to appear at Shiloh, and there he revealed himself through his word" (I Samuel 2:21, NIV).

- Second-mile leaders know that the primary way that God speaks today is through His Word. They have complete confidence in His Word and have committed themselves to being obedient to what He says to them through it.

- "The Bible, it is true, does not always give a rule for every particular course of action, and in these cases we need and must expect guidance in other ways. But the Scriptures are far more explicit, even about details, than most people think .... If, therefore, you find yourself in perplexity, first of all search and see whether the Bible speaks on the point in question, asking God to make plain to you, by the power of His Spirit, through the Scriptures, what is His mind. And whatever shall seem to you to be plainly taught here, that you must obey. No especial guidance will ever be given about a point on which the Scriptures are explicit, nor could any guidance ever be contrary to the Scriptures."[9]

- "It is essential to remember that the Bible is a book of principles, and not a book of disjointed aphorisms. Isolated texts may often be made to sanction things to which the principles of Scriptures are totally opposed. If, however, upon searching the Bible you do not find any principles that will settle your especial point of difficulty, you must then seek guidance in the other ways mentioned. God will surely voice Himself to you, either by a conviction of your judgment, or by providential circumstances, or by a clear inward impression."[10]

- "God wants you to learn to recognize His voice (John 10:27). He wants you to follow His guidance because you know His voice (John 10:v 4). His promise is, 'I will instruct you and teach you in the way you should go; I will counsel you and watch over you' (Psalm 32:8). That is why Jesus' name is Wonderful Counselor (Isaiah 9:6). That is why the Spirit is called another counselor (John 14:16)"[11]

- Second-mile leaders have learned that the Bible is the primary resource for the Holy Spirit's guidance in the major decisions of life. The more their mind is saturated with God's Word, the more prepared they are for His guidance when facing a time of crisis in their lives.

- Second-mile leaders have learned that it is more important for them to listen to God than to speak with God.

Scripture: "For the word of God is living and active. Sharper than any double-edged sword, it penetrates even to dividing soul and spirit, joints and marrow; it judges the thoughts and attitudes of the heart" (Hebrews 4:12, NIV).

Prayer: Lord, keep the ears of my heart open to hear your voice. Amen

The "Hearing God's Voice through Providential Circumstances" Principle: "The path of the righteous is like the first gleam of dawn, shining ever brighter till the full light of day" (Proverbs 4:18, NIV).

- "Circumstances are events that God uses to speak about himself and his will. We face circumstances in life every day. Unless we see God's activity in the midst of them, we will be unaware of their spiritual significance. They will simply be events in a long succession of confusing occurrences. A miracle could take place, and we would miss it. But if we are sensitive to God's voice, these same events can hold enormous significance for us. Hudson Taylor described God as 'the One Great Circumstance.'"[12]

- "Lloyd John Ogilvie says, 'God is in search of us! He wants to communicate His ultimate will and His daily guidance. As you live in the will of God, following His purposes and guidance, you find you know God better and better. As we walk in the light we receive more light; the light is brighter and shines farther (Proverbs 4:1).' As we move forward in the path already clear, God shows the next steps ahead."[13]

- "I have so many evidences of God's direction that I cannot doubt this power comes from above. I am satisfied that when the Almighty wants me to do, or not to do, any particular thing, He finds a way of letting me know it." (Abraham Lincoln)

- Second-mile leaders have learned that they can never rush God as He gives directions for the next phase of their leadership and ministry assignments. They have learned that time is never wasted while waiting on God for clear directions.

- Second-mile leaders have come to see that an open door or a closed door may or may not be a clear revelation of God's plan for their lives. However, they have come to see that they may trust God for clear instructions as to whether they should enter through a door that is opened. When considering an open door, they (like Paul) are able to say, "And after he had seen the vision, immediately we endeavored to go into Macedonia, assuredly gathering that the Lord had called us for to preach the gospel unto them" (Acts 16:10, KJV).

- Second-mile leaders have learned that as long as they don't know, they must wait. They have learned that it is always in their best interest to wait until they have clear direction, and they must remain confident that God is working for their best and for His glory. They have learned that God is more interested in making His will known to them than they are in finding it.

- Second-mile leaders must remain committed to what God has directed them to do where He has placed them until clear direction is given to a new assignment. When direction has come for the next assignment, they must demonstrate immediate obedience to move in the direction that has been revealed to them.

Scripture: "'For I know the plans I have for you,' declares the Lord, 'plans to prosper you and not to harm you, plans to give you hope and a future'" (Jeremiah 29:11, NIV).

Prayer: Lord, my prayer is that You may confirm Your direction to me through the circumstances of everyday life. Amen.

The "Hearing God's Voice through the Holy Spirit" Principle: "But when he, the Spirit of truth, comes, he will guide you into all truth, he will not speak on His own, he will speak what he hears, and he will tell you what is yet to come" (John 16:13, NIV).

- Second-mile leaders have come to depend upon the Holy Spirit as their indwelling counselor while listening to and hearing God speak to their lives. They gauge whether it is in reality God speaking to them by the inner voice of the Holy Spirit, who serves as the umpire of their hearts. "Let the peace of Christ rule in your hearts" (Colossians 3:15a, NIV).

- F. B. Meyer writes: "When you want to know the will of God three things will occur:

  1. The inward impulse

  2. The Word of God

  3. The trend of circumstances

God in the heart, impelling you forward; God in His book, corroborating whatever He says in the heart; and God in circumstances, which are always indicative of His will. Never start until these agree."

- "Grant that we may never seek to bend the straight to the crooked that is, Thy will to ours, but that we may bend the crooked to the straight, that is, our will to thine." (Augustine)

- Wesley Duewel, in his book *Let God Guide You Daily*, says that there are three levels or ways the Spirit leads us.

  1. He brings to your attention things that you would otherwise have overlooked. He directs your thoughts from within calling attention to His help. This is the more common and normal method the Spirit speaks.

  2. The Spirit leads us through the inner voice. This is not audible, but the inner awareness of a holy impression. This level of the Spirit's guidance can be frequent, but not so constant as level one.

  3. The strongest level of the Spirit's guidance is inner compulsion. "And now, compelled by the Spirit, I am going to Jerusalem, not knowing what will happen to me there" (Acts 20:22, NIV). An example of this compulsive guidance is recounted in Mark 1:12: "At once the Spirit sent him out into the desert." *Sent* in the Greek is a very strong word that means "to cast forth, with the suggestion of force, hence to drive out or force." The word suggests controlled guidance, with the Spirit gripping you.

- Second-mile leaders seek to live their lives hearing God's voice and obeying what they have been told. They seek to keep an open heart and listen to what God is saying to them and leading them to do. Constant surrender and constant obedience is their aim.

Scripture: "Since we live by the Spirit, let us keep in step with the Spirit" (Galatians 5:25, NIV).

Prayer: Lord, my prayer is that my life will be in constant step with the Holy Spirit. Amen.

The "Hearing God's Voice through a Restless Spirit" Principle: "That night the king could not sleep; so he ordered the book of the chronicles, the record of his reign, to be brought in and read to him" (Esther 6:1, NIV).

- Second-mile leaders realize that at times God brings a restless spirit within them to get their attention as to a direction that He wants them to take, a decision that He wants them to make, or a new assignment that He is about to give them.

- In my own experience, God has given me a restless spirit when things were going extremely well in the ministry where we were. I couldn't understand the "why" of the restlessness, yet I had to surrender to the Lord and simply say, "I don't understand the 'why,' but I ask that You reveal to me the 'what,' the 'where,' and the 'how.'" God has always been faithful, and I have always tried to be obedient to His direction.

- "When the time for decision has come, there need be no fear nor doubt. Where there is *submission,* a desire to do only the will of God, and *faith ,* a confidence that the Lord will guide as He has promised, there will be absolute rest of heart. Having consulted the *Word of God* and spiritually wise friends, and having earnestly sought the direction of the Holy Spirit in prayer, if circumstances and the inward peace of God unite to confirm the decision reached, that decision can confidently be accepted as the will of God. Paul's counsel is, 'Let the peace of God rule (arbitrate) in your hearts' (Colossians 3:15)."[14]

- "Just as an arbiter or umpire decides in a game, giving the deciding word on any disputed point, so the indwelling 'peace of God' umpires for us in this matter of guidance. When this inward peace is disturbed by our following some supposed guidance, then guidance is not of the Holy Spirit. When we are obeying true guidance, one of the surest tokens is peace about it in our hearts, a peace which remains undisturbed even though there may be tumult outside us …. True guidance gives peace."[15]

- "Having come to such a prayerful decision after having renounced personal preferences and prejudice, there is no reason to review or question your guidance. *Never dig up in unbelief what you have sown in faith.* Begin with the confidence that God will guide, and end with the assurance that He has guided."[16]

Scripture: "He who belongs to God hears what God says. The reason you do not hear is that you do not belong to God" (John 8:47, NIV).

Prayer: Lord, thank you for the peace that rules in my heart. May I always experience this peace through my obedience to you. Amen.

The "Hearing God's Voice through Common Sense" Principle: "And after we had seen the vision, immediately we endeavored to go into Macedonia, assuredly gathering that the Lord had called us to preach the gospel unto them" (Acts 16:10, KJV).

- Second-mile leaders like Paul act immediately when the evidence is in as to which direction they are to go and what action they are to take. Paul's struggle to know what the Lord wanted him to do is similar to today. When doors are shut to the desired direction we want to take because of the *forbidding of the Holy Spirit,* we must continue to seek God's direction as to what He has for us to do. Once the direction is given, common sense tells us to get up and go, trusting the Lord for whatever may come next.

For a number of years, I struggled with a call to world missions. After a visit from a missionary to Brazil during a World Missions Conference and a sense of release from the church where I was pastor, I made the decision to seek appointment through the then Foreign Mission Board as a missionary to Brazil. My testimony as written at the appointment service on July 14, 1966, reads: "The thought of God's call to foreign missions has been a constant companion through the years. I feel that the call has crystallized and that the time to seek appointment to foreign missions is now."

- Common sense demands that one examine the *evidence in hand.* When the evidence has been examined and all avenues have been considered, common sense will let you know whether or not you have received a genuine Macedonian call. The Holy Spirit will either confirm or deny your entering the open door.

- A common-sense approach to decision-making, of course, takes into account hearing God's voice through Scripture, providential circumstances, and confirmation through the peace that is given by the Holy Spirit's assurance that you are going in the right direction.

- Second-mile leaders base their decisions on fact, faith, and then feeling. This has been my method of determining whether or not God has spoken, or if there is something that I just feel like that I would like to do. These have been the steps in the process that I have used:

1. **Fact:** "And Hezekiah received the letter of the hand of the messengers, and read it: and Hezekiah went up into the house of the Lord and spread it out before the Lord" (II Kings 19:14 KJV). As you spread everything out before the Lord, you are able to examine the evidence as it really is, not as you would like for it to be, nor even how you may feel about it.

2. **Faith:** "Without faith it is impossible to please him: for he that cometh to God must believe that he is, and that he is a rewarder of them that diligently seek him" (Hebrews 11:6). By faith, based on the facts in hand, you may proceed in the direction that God is leading.

3. **Feeling:** "For he hath said, 'I will never leave thee, nor forsake thee.' So that we may boldly say, 'The Lord is my helper, and I will not fear what man shall do unto me'" (Hebrews 13:5b–6). God is not present because we feel it; rather, He is present because we believe in the fact of His presence. Feelings will follow faith based on the facts that have led us to make our decision to act on the evidence at hand.

Scripture: "The just shall live by faith" (Romans 1:17b).

Prayer: Lord, my prayer is that my life may be lived by faith based upon the facts of your love. Amen.

The "Biblical Leadership" Principle: "However, I consider my life worth nothing to me, if only I may finish the race and complete the task the Lord Jesus has given me; the task of testifying to the gospel of God's grace" (Acts 20:24, NIV).

- Biblical leadership always carries with it the idea of an assignment that has come from God. There is an assignment that God has given to a specific leader to accomplish a specific task.

- Paul was given the assignment of being a missionary to the Gentiles. His desire was to complete the task that had been assigned to him by Christ Himself. "But the Lord said to Ananias, 'Go! This man is my chosen instrument to carry my name before the Gentiles and their kings and before the people of Israel'" (Acts 9:15, NIV).

- Biblical leadership is not about a position to occupy, but is rather about a divine project to complete.

- Crawford Loritts, in his article "Qualities of Godly_Leadership" states, "Biblical leadership does not require a certain personality profile. You have shy, reticent people that God trusts with His assignment. You also have extroverts. You have a Gideon hiding out and God calls him a 'mighty man of valor' (Judges 6:12)."[17]

- Biblical leadership is not about how much education one has. God used farmers and fisherman as well as the very well educated—look at Peter and Paul in the Bible.

- The task of biblical leadership was given and is given to those who have a heart for God, a head that was open to His Word, and hands that were willing to take hold of the plow.

- Stephen Olford says that God is more concerned about who we are than what we do, and if who we are does not please Him, then what we do is virtually useless.

- D. L. Moody is quoted as saying, "This one thing I do—not these forty things I dabble in."

- Henry Blackaby describes spiritual leadership as moving on to God's agenda.

- An epitaph by an unknown author said, "There you stand where once was I, here I lie where soon you will be, prepare yourself to follow me." Scratched underneath were the words, "To follow you I am not content, until I know which way you went."

- Ask yourself the question, "Which way am I going?" Are you going in the direction of your choice, attempting to do God's work your way, or are you letting Him do His work through you in His way?

Scripture: "Do your best to present yourself to God as one approved, a workman who does not need to be ashamed and who correctly handles the word of truth" (II Timothy 2:15, NIV).

Prayer: Lord, my heart is open to your call and assignment. Amen.

Biblical Leadership: The "Brokenness" Principle: "Going a little farther, he fell with his face to the ground and prayed. 'My Father, if it is possible, may this cup be taken from me. Yet not as I will, but as you will'" (Matthew 26:39, NIV).

- Second-mile leaders are those that have come to understand that they are of no use to God unless there is total brokenness and complete surrender to the Lord.

- Brokenness is the first step toward possessing the qualities of a true biblical leader.

- The leadership of Moses or of Paul can easily be traced to their encounters with God that brought them to the place of true brokenness and total surrender. Their pride and self-sufficiency was completely abandoned.

- Crawford Loritts states, "Brokenness is a permanent sense of God-neediness .... When God trusts people with His assignment He first crushes them."

- Charles Spurgeon says, "When a man has failed, when he is broken and humiliated, then he sees the vanity of the world and its reward. He holds the world with a very loose hand. He wears the world as a loose garment. Now he becomes heavenly—instead of earthly—minded. The world has lost its attraction for him."

- Crawford Loritts states, "God does not use what we bring to Him, but He uses what we surrender to Him. Moses had a staff and an eighty-year-old hand. God let Moses know it is not what you have; it is Who you have that is the authority. Brokenness involves proactive surrender, and we are to give back to God what He has given us to work with."

- Nancy Leigh DeMoss contrasts proud people and broken people in an article entitled "The Heart God Revives" in the *Hearld of His Coming* as follows:

- Proud people desire to be served. Broken people are motivated to serve others.

- Proud people desire to be a success. Broken people are motivated to be faithful and to make others a success.

- Proud people have a drive to be recognized and appreciated. Broken people have a sense of their own unworthiness; they are thrilled that God would use them at all.

- Proud people have a subconscious feeling [that] "this ministry/ church is privileged to have me and my gifts"; they think of what they can do for God. Broken people's heart attitude is, "I don't deserve to have a part in any ministry"; they know that they have nothing to offer God except the life of Jesus flowing through their broken lives.[18]

- Biblical leadership is always characterized by a genuine attitude of servitude. Ron Owens, in the introduction of his book *Manley Beasley: Man of Faith—Instrument of Revival* quotes Mike Gilchrest as he describes Manley Beasley's life: "Manley was not just an instrument, he was a servant. There is a difference. An instrument is anyone God uses—whether he is right with God or not. A servant is one whose heart is set on being obedient to his master. Manley was meticulously obedient to Jesus. Pharaoh was an instrument. Paul was a servant. Manley was a servant."

Scripture: "Paul, a servant of Christ Jesus, called to be an apostle and set apart for the gospel of God" (Romans 1:1, NIV).

Prayer: Lord, my prayer is that I may always realize who you are and who I am in Christ. Amen.

Biblical Leadership: The "Accountability" Principle: "For we must all appear before the judgment seat of Christ, that each one may receive what is due him for the things done while in the body, whether good or bad" (II Corinthians 5:10, NIV),

- Second-mile leaders must always remember where they have come from and to whom they owe their debt of gratitude for the grace of God that has been extended to them.

15

- Biblical leaders carry with them a sense of deep awareness as to what their sin has cost God, what pain their sins bring to the heart of God, and the harm of their sins to His ministry on earth.

- Second-mile leaders know that there is always the danger of doing things that will place them on the shelf and disqualify them from their place of leadership.

- Biblical leadership always takes into account that "the sacrifices of God are a broken and contrite heart" (Psalm 51:17).

- Crawford Loritts states, "Your integrity to lead is found in the constant conscious realization that you have not forgotten what He forgave you of and what you are capable of doing. That is where the power and integrity to lead come from. God's assignments are always about Him, and He does not want some obnoxious, arrogant person competing for His glory."

Scripture: "What a wretched man I am! Who will rescue me from this body of death? Thanks be to God, through Jesus Christ our Lord! So then, I myself in mind am a slave to God's law, but in the sinful nature a slave to the law of sin" (Romans 7:24–25).

Prayer: Lord, may I always be reminded that I am accountable to you. Amen.

Biblical Leadership: The "Gap" Principle: "Not that I have already reached the goal or am already fully mature, but I make every effort to take hold of it because I have been taken hold of by Christ Jesus" (Philippians 3:12, HCSB).

- Biblical leadership begins in the heart of those called to lead. Biblical leaders have a sense of inadequacy for the task to which they are being called.

- Crawford Loritts states, "David realized that he was too small to wear Saul's armor. God would take him from where he was and make him into what he wanted him to be. God was teaching him that 'I am the God of the gap.' "

- Crawford Loritts is quoted as saying, "God never separates His assignments from the sanctifying process of the leader. So the leader authentically not only speaks about where things need to be, but he is a picture of where things need to be. That is the reason why there is always a horrendous gap between what God tells you and where you are." [19]

- "Do not pray for tasks equal to your powers. Pray for powers equal to your task. Then the doing of your work shall be no miracle, but you shall be the miracle." (Phillip Brooks)

- The biblical call to leadership results in the called being willing to accept the challenge of the call without demanding all the details of the plan that God has in mind. The person who has been called is content to *sail with orders sealed.*

- Crawford Loritts states, "God gave Moses enough to know what to say to Pharaoh, but he did not tell him all that was going to happen. God told Moses that when they got into the wilderness, He was going to give a cloud and a pillar and every day they were going to have to seek God for direction (Exodus 33:7–8)."

- Second-mile leadership accepts the fact that sometimes one may feel that they are in *over their head.* Yet their trust in God for His direction for the next step never wavers.

- It is true that God is fully capable in His ability to *equip* those whom He calls.

- God's way is to *equip the called* rather than *calling the equipped.*

- Crawford Loritts says, "But the very nature of God's call is in the gap between what He is asking and in what you feel you are able to do. God makes His person through the callings that He gives them."

- In his article, "Qualities of Godly Leadership," Crawford Loritts states that there are four jewels in the leader's development that God uses consistently—besides the magnitude of the assignment—to keep us running back to His presence.

(1) The first one is failure .... Failure is often a part of God's plan ... we need to examine our failures.

(2) Secondly, He uses personal struggles .... Your struggles are not necessarily disqualifiers, although sin is (II Corinthians 12:9).

(3) Thirdly, suffering .... Suffering brings a heart connection to people that nothing else can do. It is a part of the journey of life. It helps you not to be condescending and arrogant.

(4) Fourth, success through hardship ... The work of God is not easy. Paul told Timothy to endure hardship, to stop whining, to watch his priorities, and to not get entangled with the things of this life. The real fruit of the ministry comes from your endurance. (Loritts)[20]

Scripture: "He who calls you is faithful, who will also do it" (I Thessalonians 5:24, (HCSB).

Prayer: Lord, make me into who you want me to be so that I may allow you to do through me all that you want to do. Amen.

Biblical Leadership: The "Servanthood" Principle: "Jesus called them together and said, 'You know that the rulers of the Gentiles lord it over them, and their high officials exercise authority over them. Not so with you. Instead whoever wants to become great among you must be your servant, and whoever wants to be first must be your slave, just as the Son of Man did not come to be served, but to serve, and to give his life as a ransom for many' " (Matthew 20:26–28).

- Jesus clearly taught that biblical leadership was first and foremost about acts and attitudes of service.

- "The journey of life is to move from a self-serving heart to a serving heart. You finally become an adult when you realize that life is about what you give, rather than what you get." (Ken Blanchard)

- Biblical leadership is never seen as *self-serving*. It is always seen as serving others.

- " 'Whoever wants to hold the first positions among you must be everybody's slave. For the Son of Man did not come to be served but to serve and to give His life a ransom' (C. B. Williams, Mark 10:44–45). Each of the heroes of faith immortalized in Hebrews 11 was called to sacrifice as well as to service."[21]

- "Biblically we serve because we are servants. We give out of the identity of serving. In the Bible, as I said earlier, leadership is not spoken of as a position. The position is given as a platform to serve. You are not given a position of leadership because *you paid your dues*. You are not given a position of leadership just to occupy a bigger office. The only reason why you lead biblically is because God can trust you to serve. It is all about the assignment and the service." (Crawford Loritts)

- "The final estimate of men shows that history cares not an iota for the rank or title a man has borne, or the office he has held, but only the quality of his deeds and the character of his mind and heart." (Samuel Logan Brengle)

- "The world cannot always understand one's profession of faith, but it can understand service." (Ian Maclaren)

- "God walks with the humble; he reveals himself to the lowly; he gives understanding to the little ones; he discloses his meaning to pure minds, but hides his grace from the curious and proud." (Thomas à Kempis)

- Wesley Duewel says, "Measure your life, not by how much you get, but how much you give. Measure your life by the extent to which you put God first, others second, and self last."

- "Nothing is more important in a leader's life and ministry than to lead an exemplary life in all things. His leadership can be no more effective than his life. His manner of living prepares the way for the reception of his words. The example of your life validates or invalidates your ministry. You have no more credibility in any community than your life warrants. You must incarnate what you say. You must demonstrate that the gospel is true."[22]

Scripture: "Should you then seek great things for yourself? Seek them not" (Jeremiah 45:5a, NIV).

Prayer: Lord, my prayer is that I will hear you say, "Well done, good and faithful servant." Amen.

Biblical Leadership: The "Obedience" Principle: "After removing Saul, he made David their king. He testified concerning him: 'I have found David son of Jesse a man after my own heart; he will do everything I want him to do' " (Acts 13:22, NIV).

- Biblical leadership is characterized by instant obedience. When God has revealed a certain course of action to be taken, there is a willingness to act without doubt or debate.

- David was willing to obey God in every instance and is described as a man after the heart of God because of willing obedience.

- Paul was willing to obey the Macedonian call. "After Paul had seen the vision, we got ready at once to leave for Macedonia, concluding that God had called us to preach the gospel to them" (Acts 16:10).

- Crawford Loritts says, "Every man or woman of God who has been trusted with God's assignments has been characterized by radical, immediate obedience."

- "I'm going to take the pressure off of every one of you. None of you has to be successful, but you have to be obedient." (Bill Bright)

- In Wesley Duewel's book, *Measure Your Life,* he writes that you are responsible for two forms of obedience: "Obedience to God's general commands and obedience to God's personalized commands. God's requirements, as taught in His Word, are for every person. You are responsible to obey them. You need no further guidance if it is in God's Word. That settles it …. Some of God's requirements, on the other hand, are very personal. God may give you personal convictions about things. It is the obedience He requires of you, not of everyone. He may call you to missionary service, to special sacrificial giving of His kingdom, to a specific amount of time in prayer. He may not require these of others. They are God's personal guidance to you."

- "To know God's will is life's greatest treasure. To do God's will is life's greatest pleasure." (Unknown)

- "It is a greater thing to obey the Word of the Lord than to preach it." (Unknown)

- "I'll go where you want me to go, dear Lord,
  O'er mountain or plain or sea;
  I'll say what you want me to say, dear Lord,
  I'll be what you want me to be"[23]

- The words of the old hymn puts everything into perspective—there is no other way "to be happy in Jesus than to trust and obey."

Scripture: "To obey is better than sacrifice, and to hearken than the fat of rams" (I Samuel 15:22).

Prayer: Lord, my prayer is that I may be known as one after your heart because of my total obedience to you in all things. Amen.

Section Two
The Character of a Second-Mile Leader

The "Heart" Principle: "The Lord has sought out a man after his own heart and appointed him leader of his people" (I Samuel 13:14b, NIV).

- Second-mile leaders are known for their hearts that are ablaze with love for God and a genuine love for people. "As water reflects a face, so a man's heart reflects the man" (Proverbs 27:19, NIV).

- Henry Blackaby is quoted as saying, "Each man God used had a responsive heart ready to hear God and a life that was available to obey God. Each possessed the integrity to honor God."

- "God, the church, and the world are looking for men with burning hearts, hearts filled with love of God; filled with compassion for the ills of the church and the world; filled with passion for the glory of God, the gospel of Jesus Christ, and the salvation of the lost." (Dr. George W. Peters)

- "It takes more than a busy church, a friendly church, or even an evangelical church to impact a community for Christ. It must be a church ablaze, led by leaders who are ablaze for God."[24]

- John Wesley, evangelist of the burning heart, was reportedly asked by a fellow minister how to gain an audience. He replied, "If the preacher will burn, others will come to see the fire."

- Second-mile leaders know that passionless Christianity will not put out the fires of hell. The best way to fight a raging fire is with fire. A passionless leader will never set the people ablaze.

- Second-mile leaders are determined to *guard their hearts,* taking the challenge of Proverbs 4:23 personally: "Above all else, guard your heart, for it is the wellspring of life." They understand that their hearts are the source of life-giving water and motivation for leadership.

- "The effective leaders I have met, worked with, and observed behaved in much the same way … they made sure that the person they saw in the mirror in the morning was the kind of person they wanted to be, respect, and believe in. They fortified themselves against the leader's greatest temptations; do things that are popular rather than right, and do petty, mean, sleazy things.

Scripture: "Create in me a clean heart, O God, and renew a right spirit within me" (Psalm 51:10).

Prayer: Lord, my prayer is that you might set my heart ablaze with a holy zeal to reach the lost and encourage the saved for a great, heaven-sent revival. Amen.

The "Above All Else" Principle: "Above all else, guard your heart, for it is the wellspring of life" (Proverbs 4:23, NIV).

- Second-mile leaders are very aware that their hearts are where the life of their leadership begins and ends. Their hearts are overflowing with the love of God or stagnant pools of their own selfish motives.

- One's character is either developed or destroyed in the heart. The writer of Proverbs gives these instructions: "Keep vigilant watch over your heart; that's where life starts. Don't talk out of both sides of your mouth; avoid careless banter, white lies, and gossip. Keep your eyes straight ahead; ignore all sideshow distractions. Watch your step, and the road will stretch out smooth before you. Look neither right nor left; leave evil in the dust (Proverbs 4:23–27, *The Message*).

- "God is more concerned about who we are than what we do, and if who we are does not please Him, then what we do is virtually useless." (Stephen Olford)

- "Would you know who is the greatest saint in the world? It is not he who prays most or fasts most; it is not he who gives most alms or is the most eminent for temperance, chastity, or justice; but it is he who is always thankful to God, who wills everything that God wills, who receives everything as an instance of God's goodness and has a heart always ready to praise God for it." (William Law)

- "Guarding your heart means to put a hedge of protection around it because it is the *wellspring of life,* the source of life-giving water."[25]

- When the "Above All Else" principle is applied, your heart is well guarded so that nothing will be allowed to poison, pollute, or dilute your passion for Christ and what He desires to do through your life.

- "Make the service of Christ the business of your life, the will of Christ the law of your life, the presence of Christ the joy of your life, and the glory of Christ the crown of your life." (Church Bulletin Cover 9/8/96)

Scripture: "Create in me a pure heart, O God, and renew a steadfast spirit within me" (Psalm 51:10, NIV).

Prayer: Lord, above all else, guard my heart, that I may not sin against thee. Amen.

The "Brokenness" Principle: "But rather offer yourselves to God, as those who have been brought from death to life; and offer the parts of your body to him as instruments of righteousness" (Romans 6:13b, NIV).

- Second-mile leaders realize that the problem of victory is within, not without. When you are broken in your will, God can accomplish His purpose through you.

- Before God can work through you, He must work with you and in you to bring you to a place of complete submission to Him.

- Paul Billheimer says, "Whole, unbruised, unbroken men are of little use to God. You can't separate effective service from brokenness."

- After many years of working for the Lord and attempting to do the Lord's work my way, I came to realize that this was not the way the Lord wanted to get His work done. Rather, He wanted to do His work through me. I needed to be in submission to him in order that He could do His work through me.

- My prayer was something like this as I came to the place of brokenness: "I have come to the place in my life that in everything I can say, 'For better or worse, for richer or poorer, missionary, pastor, evangelist, large church or small, I have no desire for my own life, but am perfectly willing to do the will of God.'" This is a prayer and a commitment that I first said on September 12, 1972—and a prayer I am constantly reminded to voice.

- Second-mile leaders understand that brokenness is essential to their being blessed and being a blessing. A refusal to be broken will place you on the shelf—and there are no happy people on the shelf.

- Second-mile leaders realize that the problem of victory and continuous revival is within, not without. When you are broken in your will, God can accomplish His purpose through you.

Scripture: "The sacrifices of God are a broken spirit; a broken and contrite heart, O God, you will not despise" (Psalm 51:17, NIV).

Prayer: Lord, my prayer is that I may always be in total submission to you. Amen.

The "Lord's Cup" Principle: "'What do you want me to do for you?' He asked. They replied, 'Let us sit at your right hand and the other at your left hand in your glory.' 'You don't know what you are asking,' Jesus said. 'Can you drink the cup I drink or be baptized with the baptism I am baptized with?'" (Mark 10:36–38, NIV).

- Second-mile leaders must understand that *position and power are not for the asking, but for or by drinking the cup and receiving the baptism.*

- "No one need aspire to leadership in the work of God who is not prepared to pay a price greater than his contemporaries and colleagues are willing to pay. True leadership always exacts a heavy toll on the whole man, and the more effective the leadership is, the higher the price to be paid."[26]

- It has been said that a cross stands in the way of spiritual leadership—a cross upon which the leader must consent to be impaled. [27]

- Second-mile leaders have accepted the *cup of life* that God has dealt them. They know that the drinking of their cup will either bring a blessing or bitterness, dependent upon their acceptance of it. The cup is a metaphor of life and experience that God hands out to men.

- The Lord's cup meant Gethsemane and Calvary for Christ (Matthew 26:39; John 18:11). His concern was whether or not the cup was God's will. His drinking the cup meant His submission to and obedience of God's will for His life.

- Second-mile leaders have yielded their lives completely to the Lord. This is the Lord's cup for them. They understand that before doing the will of God, they must first be subject to God's authority in their lives.

- One is not broken until all resentment and rebellion against God is removed. Until one is broken, he is still full of himself and his plans. It has been said that whole, unbruised, unbroken people are of little use to God.

- The Lord's cup is total obedience to the authority and will of God in your life (Matthew 26:39; John 18:11).

Scripture: "I am crucified with Christ: nevertheless I live; yet not I but Christ liveth in me: and the life which I now live in the flesh I live by the faith of the Son of God, who loved me, and gave himself for me" (Galatians 2:20, KJV).

Prayer: Lord, my prayer is one of submission in every area of my life. I am perfectly willing to do your will. Amen.

The "Lord's Baptism" Principle: "'What do you want me to do for you?' He asked. They replied, 'Let us sit at your right hand and the other at your left hand in your glory.' 'You don't know what you are asking,' Jesus said. 'Can you drink the cup I drink or be baptized with the baptism I am baptized with?'" (Mark 10:36–38, NIV)

- In Luke 12:50, Jesus speaks of a future baptism that he must undergo: "But I have a baptism to undergo, and how distressed I am until it is completed." Christ was anticipating a release of himself. The fullness of the glory of God was bound up in an incarnate body. The cross is there for the release of life as well as the atonement for sin. God releases his life through the cross.

- Baptism is first death; then it is life released. We must have the outer person broken so that the inner person may flow out. It is when the grain of wheat falls into the ground and has burst that life begins to flow.

- Jesus says, "The baptism which I will receive will break open my outer shell and release life ... are you willing to be so baptized?" (John 12:24–26)

- The Lord seems to be saying to James and John, "Since you ask to be different from the rest by sitting on my right and left, are you able to be distinct from the rest of God's children? You must drink the cup and be baptized before you can sit at my right and left in glory."

- A refusal to be broken will place you on the shelf—there are no happy people on the shelf.

- The baptism is a picture of the death and resurrection—a life of freedom, power, and love.

Scripture: "In the same way, count yourselves dead to sin but alive to God in Christ Jesus. Therefore do not let sin reign in your mortal body so that you obey its evil desires. Do not offer the parts of your body to sin, as instruments of wickedness, but rather offer yourselves to God, as those who have been brought from death to life; and offer the parts of your body to him as instruments of righteousness" (Romans 6:11–13, NIV).

Prayer: Lord, I now submit my life to your cup and your baptism. Amen.

The "Water Boy" Principle: "An officer of the king of Israel answered, Elisha son of Shaphat is here, He used to pour water on the hands of Elijah" (II Kings 3:11, NIV).

- Second-mile leaders understand the importance of being faithful in what might be considered the small things of life—such as pouring water on the hands of someone like Elijah.

- Our faithfulness over small things is necessary before larger responsibilities are given in God's kingdom enterprise.

- "The Lord doesn't catapult us into greatness. He grows us into spiritual maturity. He stretches us slowly so that we don't break. He causes us to grow slowly so that we stay balanced. The unfolding of God's plan for our lives is a process that is lifelong." (Unknown)

- "Learn the lesson that, if you are to do the work of a prophet, what you need is not a scepter but a hoe." (Bernard of Clairvaux)

- "A Christian is a perfectly free lord of all, subject to none. A Christian is a perfectly dutiful servant of all, subject to all." (Martin Luther)

- "The cross-life is the life of voluntary submission. The cross-life is the life of freely accepted servanthood." (Richard Foster)

- More than 100 years ago, C. I. Scofield wrote of "Three Tests of Preachers" (Psalm 75:4–7):

    1. The Test of Obscurity leads you to whine—be careful not to whine about where God has placed you.

    2. The Test of Applause leads you to be proud.

    3. The Test of Suffering leads you to quit.

Scripture: "His master replied, 'Well done, good and faithful servant! You have been faithful with a few things; I will put you in charge of many things. Come and share your master's happiness!'" (Matthew 25:21)

Prayer: Lord, help me to always keep in mind that I am your water boy—use me as you will. Amen.

The "Ittai" Principle: "But Ittai replied to the king, 'As surely as the Lord lives, and as my lord the king lives, wherever my lord the king may be, whether it means life or death, there will your servant be'" (II Samuel 15:21, NIV).

- Second-mile leaders give undivided allegiance to their king, Jesus. The Ittai principle simply means that you are committed to the service of Christ—no matter what the cost. It means that you are willing to go wherever he leads you and do whatever he says. Your loyalty is without exception—whatever the cost to you personally. You are a faithful servant to the King of Kings and Lord of Lords.

- Second-mile leaders need to be reminded that faithfulness is theirs to give, and success is God's to give.

- Second-mile leaders must remember that faithfulness is more important than fruitfulness.

- "Trust and Obey" is not merely just the name of a hymn—it is the key to the advancement of God's kingdom. Wesley Duewel says, "God's Kingdom advances on the feet, the words, the prayers, and all the obedience of God's children." A Christian poet has written:

> God has no hands but our hands
> To do His work today.
> He has no feet but our feet
> To lead men in His way.
> He has no tongue but our tongue
> To tell men how He died.
> He has no help but our help
> To lead them to His side[28]

- Second-mile leaders understand the Ittai principle, and they are committed to faithfulness. "So then, men ought to regard us as servants of Christ and those entrusted with the secret things of God. Now it is required that those who have been given a trust must prove faithful" (I Corinthians 4:1–2, NIV).

Scripture: "His master replied, 'Well done, good and faithful servant! You have been faithful with a few things; I will put you in charge of many things. Come and share in your master's happiness'" (Matthew 25:21, NIV).

Prayer: Lord, my prayer is that I may be found faithful to you in all that you have entrusted me to do. Amen.

"The Thorn" Principle: "To keep me from becoming conceited … there was given me a thorn in my flesh, a messenger of Satan to torment me" (II Corinthians 12:7, NIV).

- Second-mile leaders such as Paul accept the thorns in order to be more useful in God's kingdom. God used the thorn to keep Paul from spiritual pride and self-exaltation. Paul could not have had the revelations without the thorn.

- Second-mile leaders learn to accept the thorns of life and use them to be more dependent on the grace and power of God in their lives rather than their own abilities and energies. They come to realize that God's power is made perfect in their weakness.

- Watchman Nee says ," We seldom learn anything new about God except through adversity."

- Alexander Maclaren says, " Every affliction comes with a message from God."

- "God has something to say in our afflictions and the essential thing is to get quiet enough to hear God's voice. Someone has said that one of the severest tests of character is the ability to wait upon God without losing patience with him."[29]

- "Until you have learned to face, overcome, and utilize adversity, you are dangerously vulnerable, because, Paul tells us in Acts 14:22, 'we must through tribulation enter the kingdom of God.' We cannot avoid tribulation, adversity, and affliction, but if we understand that these things may be good, that nothing intrinsically evil can come to a child of God, that only a wrong reaction can injure him; if he learns how to utilize his problems for spiritual growth, then he has it made. If God's blessings are for our good and if Satan's assaults are transformed into blessings by our reaction, we have nothing to fear because everything is working for our good."[30]

- "It is doubtful that anyone reaches truly great sainthood without suffering, and at times the greatest saints have been the greatest sufferers. At present we are not what we should be, neither are we what they shall be. But God does not work without a pattern or design. He knows what He is doing. There is a hand guiding and controlling these circumstances." [31]

Scripture: "But he said to me, 'My grace is sufficient for you, for my power is made perfect in weakness. Therefore I will boast all the more gladly about my weaknesses, so that Christ's power may rest on me'" (II Corinthians 12:9, NIV).

Prayer: Lord, thank you for the thorns that have been placed in my life. Help me to accept them and utilize them for the glory of God. Amen.

The "Scar" Principle: "Finally, let no one cause me trouble, for I bear on my body the marks of Jesus" (Galatians 6:17).

- Dr. Samuel M. Zwemer recalls the striking fact that the only thing Jesus took pains to show after His resurrection was His scars—He showed His disciples his hands and his side.

- Scars are authentic marks of faithful discipleship and true spiritual leadership. Nothing moves people more than the print of the nails and the mark of the spear.

- In the book *Finishing Strong,* author Steve Farrar notes, "It means that you are a man who has fought some battles for the kingdom and has the scars to prove it."

  > Out of the presses of pain
  > Cometh the soul's best wine;
  > And the eyes that have shed no rain
  > Can shed but little shine.[32]

- "Therefore a lifetime of sorrows, anguish, and disappointments is required to transform one into the lofty likeness of the Lord, to lead him into advanced degrees of maturity in Christlikeness and agape love."[33]

- "Even if there is an easy way to get to heaven, I am not sure I would be comfortable there without any battle scars." (Paul Billheimer)

- "If God is going to entrust any of us with responsibility in His work, He may have to take us also through discipline by which we are broken regarding earth and its comforts and joys."[34]

- "Tribulation's imprint is on all great saints. It has been said that crowns are cast in crucibles, and chains of character that wind about the feet of God are forged in earthly flames."[35]

Scripture: "Surely it was for my benefit that I suffered such anguish" (Isaiah 38:17).

Prayer: Lord, help me to be willing to submit to your will—no matter the scars that submission may bring. Amen.

The "Tear" Principle: "Serving the Lord with all humility of mind, and with many tears" (Acts 20:19a, KJV).

- Second-mile leaders serve with humility and with tears, knowing that they are indeed unworthy to be in the place of leadership that has been assigned to them by the divine direction of God. They have a deep concern for the challenge that is before them and are brought to tears of compassion for those they serve.

- Second-mile leaders are known for their tears. They embrace the saying, "People don't care how much you know until they know how much you care." "Therefore watch and remember, that by the space of three years I ceased not to warn everyone night and day with tears" (Acts 20:31).

- "A compassionless Christianity drifts into ceremonialism and formalism and dries up the fountains of life and causes the world to commit spiritual suicide. A compassionate leadership in the Christian movements of the world is now our greatest need. Every niche of the world needs the ministry of a fired soul, burning and shining, blood-hot with the zeal and conviction of a conquering gospel. Many a minister is on a treadmill, marking time, drying up, living a professional life, without power, nor earning his salt because he has no passion for God or souls and no power for effective service. May our God kindle Holy fires of evangelism in all churches and pulpits where such is needed." (L. R. Scarbrough) [36]

- Second-mile leaders know that tears are still a pressing need in our day. General Booth received a message from one of his captains that the work was so hard he could make no progress. The reply was, "Try tears."

- It has been said that a lost burden is one of the greatest tragedies that possibly can come to a Christian's life. It seems an ordinary thing to hear someone say, "I don't have a burden for souls like I used to have." Paul, a great second-mile leader, gives us this challenge: "I say the truth in Christ, I lie not, my conscience also bearing me witness in the Holy Ghost, that I have great heaviness and continual sorrow in my heart. For I could wish myself accursed from Christ for my brethren" (Romans 9:1–3).

- I am reminded of a great second-mile leader, Pastor Eleterio Rocha of Brazil. More than fifty pastors came from the small country church where he served as pastor for more than fifty years. Each one of them shared his burden: *"Minha patria para Cristo—eis a minha peticao,"* which means, "My country for Christ—this is my fervent prayer."

- Second-mile leaders must have prayers that are bathed in tears that flow from desperate hearts—prayers that flow from hearts that are totally serving the Lord. We must have a burden that brings tears from hearts that are broken over the condition of the lost. We must be awakened to the principle of tears.

> One man awake, can awaken another
> The second can waken his next door brother
> The three awake, can rouse a town
> By turning the whole place upside down.
> The many awake, can make such a fuss
> That it finally awakens the rest of us.
> One man up, with dawn in his eyes, multiplies.[37]

Scripture: "They that sow in tears shall reap in joy. He that goeth forth and weepeth, bearing precious seed, shall doubtless come again rejoicing bringing his sheaves with him" (Psalm 126:5–6).

Prayer: Lord, may I be burdened to the point of tears for those who do not know You and those who are not living for You. Amen.

The "Quarry" Principle: "And the temple, when it was being built, was built with stone finished at the quarry, so that no hammer or chisel or any iron tool was heard in the temple while it was being built" (I Kings 6:7, NKJV).

- Second-mile leaders always keep in mind that their lives are a work in progress, as God is continually working to mold and shape their lives so that they will bring the most glory to Him.

- The building of Solomon's temple illustrates this principle. Every stone that went into that amazing structure was hewn to such exact specifications at the quarry site that each stone fit perfectly into the place for which it was designed.

- "All true believers in all ages are the living stones in that heavenly temple, and God is preparing them in His quarry down here, amid the noise and tumult of earth, each for his place in His temple above." (A. N. Hodgin)

- "God is much more interested in what we are than in what we do, in what we become than in what we achieve." (Paul Billheimer)

- Quarry stones are insensitive, but the living stones with which God is working are not. This means that God cannot shape without pain. Where there is no pain, no shaping is achieved. The tools He must use are sharp and abrasive. Quarry stones cannot resist, but the *living* stones may.

- "You also, like living stones, are being built into a spiritual house to be a holy priesthood, offering spiritual sacrifices acceptable to God through Jesus Christ" (I Peter 2:5, NIV).

- We need to be reminded that God is still making us. We are being *conformed in the image of Christ.* He is at work on us with a mallet and chisel, like a master sculptor working on a piece of stone.

- "At present we are not what we should be, neither are we what we shall be. But God does not work without a pattern or design. He knows what He is doing regardless of our blindness. There is nothing accidental about the providences that come into our lives."[38]

- How can we ever be discouraged and frustrated when we already share the glory of God? Our suffering today only guarantees more glory when Christ returns.

  > "The Weaver"
  > My life is but a weaving
  > between my Lord and me,
  > I cannot choose
  > the colors He worketh steadly.

Oftimes he weaveth sorrow,
and I in foolish pride
forget He sees
the upper and I, the underside.
Not till the loom is silent,
And the shuttles cease to fly,
Shall God unroll the canvas
And explain the reason why.
The dark threads are as needful
in the Weaver's skillful hand
As the threads of gold and silver
In the pattern He has planned.
(Author Unknown)[39]

Scripture: "For I will show him how great things he must suffer for my name's sake" (Acts 9:16,KJV).

Prayer: Lord, help me to always be pliable in your hands as you work in my life for my greater good and your greater glory. Amen.

The "River" Principle: "But whoever drinks from the water that I will give him will never get thirsty again, ever! In fact, the water I will give him will become a well of water springing up within him for eternal life" (John 4:14, HCSB).

- A second-mile leader's life certainly can be compared to a river. "There is a river whose streams make glad the city of God, the holy place where the Most High dwells" (Psalm 46:4, NIV).

- "A river touches places of which its source knows nothing, and Jesus says if we have received of His fullness, however small the visible measure of our lives, out of us will flow the rivers that will bless to the uttermost parts of the earth. We have nothing to do with the outflow. This is the work of God that you believe ... God rarely allows a soul to see how great a blessing he is." (Oswald Chambers)[40]

- The overflow from your life has great influence on those who are the closest to you. Your family is either blessed by your life or made bitter by your attitude and actions.

37

- Your life touches those with whom you come in contact. Many times you are not aware of the influence that you have on those who are around you.

- Your life's influence extends from generation to generation.

- "One generation plants the trees, and the next generation enjoys the shade." (Unknown)

- Your life casts a very long shadow.

- "Every generation must stand on the shoulders of the previous generation and reach higher." (St. Augustine)

- It has been said of the church that it should be a river of God's blessings, not a reservoir. The same can be said of one's life—you should never allow your life to just be a reservoir of God's blessings, but should determine that your life will be a river of His blessings, allowing His love to pass through you to touch those with whom you come in contact.

- "A loving person lives in a loving world. A hostile person lives in a hostile world. Everyone you meet is your mirror." (Ken Keyes, Jr.)

- "Don't judge each day by the harvest you reap but by the seeds you plant." (Robert Louis Stevenson)

- "Character is made in the small moments of our lives." (Phillip Brooks)

- "A life isn't significant except for its impact on other lives." (Jackie Robinson)

- "Every man is a hero and an oracle to somebody, and to that person, whatever he says has an enhanced value." (Ralph Waldo Emerson)

Scripture: "Praise be to the God and Father of our Lord Jesus Christ, the Father of compassion and the God of all comfort, who comforts us in all our troubles, so that we can comfort those in any trouble with the comfort we ourselves have received from God" (II Corinthians 1:3, NIV).

Prayer: Lord, may my life have the kind of influence that is like refreshing streams of water for all that it touches. Amen.

Section Three
The Commitment of a Second-Mile Leader

The "Commitment" Principle: "If anyone would come after me, he must deny himself and take up his cross daily and follow me" (Luke 9:23, NIV).

- Second-mile leaders have come to grips with the demands of Jesus. Their commitment to following Him is concrete, constant, and complete.

> Give me a man of God, one man,
> Whose faith is a master of his mind,
> And I will right all wrongs
> And bless the name of all mankind.
>
> Give me a man of God, one man,
> Whose tongue is touched with heaven's fire,
> And I will flame the darkest hearts
> With high resolve and clean desire.
>
> Give me a man of God, one man,
> One mighty prophet of the Lord,
> And I will give you peace on earth,
> Bought with a prayer and not a sword.
>
> Give me a man of God, one man,
> True to the vision that he sees,
> And I will build your broken shrines
> And bring the nations to their knees.
> (George Liddell)[41]

- The Bible frequently says that God is searching for someone who is completely committed to him—one person *after His own heart,* one person *to stand in the gap,* one person who will completely obey Him and stand firm in all things. God is looking for those who will be second-mile leaders.

Scripture: "And anyone who does not take his cross and follow me is not worthy of me" (Matthew 10:38, NIV).

Prayer: Lord, my prayer is that I may be a person who is totally committed to you in all ways. Amen.

The "Paul" Principle: "Brothers, I do not consider myself to have taken hold of it. But one thing I do: Forgetting what is behind and straining toward what is ahead, I press on toward the goal to win the prize to which God has called me heavenward in Christ Jesus" (Philippians 3:13–14, NIV).

- The Paul principle is demonstrated through the passion of Paul's own words in Philippians 3:13–14. Paul was able to keep things in their proper perspective—"forgetting what was behind and focusing on the future … straining toward what is ahead."

- Paul was able to forget what was behind him and keep his focus on the future. What was done was done. What had happened had happened. He had no control over the past events of his life. He had not allowed—and would not allow—a root of bitterness to grow in his life. He had the grace to forgive and move on with his life.

- Paul understood that *living in the past* would not allow him to have *any future.*

- Paul was not willing to rest on past accomplishments, because he was not willing to slack off, as some would do—the thought of heaven, of meeting Christ face-to-face, caused him to *strain toward what was ahead.*

- Second-mile leaders must be able to leave the past in the past and focus on what God desires to do through their lives in the present and future.

- Second-mile leaders identify with the old saying, "If you always do what you've always done, then you will always get what you've always gotten." While you may learn from past failures, never allow them to become your focus—keep your focus on the future and move on with life.

- Second-mile leaders never are satisfied living in the past, nor do they think that they have done all they can do. There is always another challenge—another mountain to climb.

    "Higher Ground"
    I'm pressing on the upward way,
    New heights I'm gaining everyday

Still praying as I'm on-ward bound,
Lord plant my feet on higher ground."
(Johnson Oatman Jr.)[42]

Scripture: "However I consider my life worth nothing to me, if only I may finish the race and complete the task the Lord Jesus has given me, the task of testifying to the gospel of God's grace" (Acts 20:24, NIV).

Prayer: Lord, my prayer is that my focus will always be on you and what you desire to be and do through my life. Amen.

The "Leading from the Book" Principle: "All Scripture is God-breathed and is useful for teaching, rebuking, correcting, and training in righteousness ... preach the word, be prepared in season and out of season; correct, rebuke and encourage with great patience and careful instruction" (II Timothy 3:16, 4:2, NIV).

- John Wesley, the itinerant preacher, carried in his buggy a wide selection of classical literature and medical journals. Even though he was widely read, he was known as "a man of one book." Our authority comes from one book—the Bible.

- "The man who feeds upon God's Word will become strong; the one who neglects it will be dwarfed. Both stature and strength are gauged by the quality of spiritual food eaten and assimilated. Wherever you find a spiritual anemic the reason is improper food."[43]

- "Sometimes a Christian worker has lost his power for no other reason than neglect of the Bible. Because of this, his message is devoid of freshness and fruitfulness. The inevitable result is the giving of his own word in the wisdom, eloquence and energy of the flesh. This God never promises to bless."[44]

- "Jesus stood out in His day because *he taught as one who had authority* (Matthew 7:29). In today's milieu of religious pluralism, the Christian leader will command attention; especially if he believes Scripture is absolute truth in all that it addresses."[45]

- God's Word is the only guidebook that we have for an effective, efficient, and lasting ministry.

Scripture: "For the word of God is living and active. Sharper than any double-edged sword, it penetrates even to dividing soul and spirit, joints and marrow; it judges the thoughts and attitudes of the heart" (Hebrews 4:12, NIV).

Prayer: Lord, may I be known as a person immersed in the Bible as I proclaim it and live it. Amen.

"The Secret Place" Principle: "But when you pray, go into your room, close the door and pray to the Father...who sees what is done in secret and He will reward you." (Matthew 6:6, NIV).

- Jesus talked of the closet or secret place of prayer. He talked of a level of commitment to God that was only known by God—the kind of prayer that one prays when no one else is looking and is alone with God.

- The secret place is where the person of God is alone with God to get a word from God for the people of God.

- The Secret Place is where the Man of God goes to talk to God about the needs of his people and prepares to talk to his people about God. [46]"Talking to men for God is a great thing, but talking to God for men is greater still. Your prayer life is a clear revelation of how much a person of God and how much a spiritual leader you are." (E. M. Bounds)

- Great praying is a characteristic of God's great leaders, . What should be the role of prayer in your life as a Christian leader? The answer should be the same as that of the early apostles. They decided to give themselves to two things: "We will give our attention to prayer and the ministry of the word (Acts 6:4). For them, prayer was the first priority.

- The secret place is where the person of God goes to sit before the Lord: "Then King David went in and sat before the Lord" (II Samuel 7:18, NIV).

- Sitting before the Lord in the secret place will shape your own life, sharpen your spiritual weapons, saturate your heart with compassion, separate the important from the non-important, simplify life's complexities, and replace your dependence on self with a dependence on God.

- A second-mile leader is known as one who leads from their knees.

Scripture: "One day Jesus was praying in a certain place. When he finished, one of his disciples said to him, 'Lord teach us to pray, just as John taught his disciples'" (Luke 11:1, NIV).

Prayer: Lord, it is my prayer that my talk will match my walk and that I will be known as one who truly leads from their knees. Amen.

The "Leading through Conflict" Principle: "They had such a sharp disagreement that they parted company. Barnabas took Mark and sailed for Cyprus" (Acts 15:39, NIV). "I plead with Euodia and I plead with Syntyche to agree with each other in the Lord. Yes, I ask you loyal yokefellow, help these women who have contended at my side in the cause of the gospel, along with Clement and the rest of my fellow workers, whose names are in the book of life" (Philippians 4:2–3, NIV).

- Conflict is inevitable. When—not if—conflict occurs, your leadership will be challenged. Conflict can be God's way of keeping you dependant on Him.

- Satan doesn't seem to bother about any church much until it begins to invade his territory.

- Satan knows that ministry shuts down when he is able to persuade leaders to focus on problems rather than possibilities.

- You can't wait for the storm to blow over—you've got to learn to work in the rain.

- Remember, the conflict is spiritual, not carnal (II Corinthians 10:3–5). If their criticism and provocations tend to get under your skin, this should remind you that the struggle is not flesh and blood, but spiritual. The weapons of your warfare must always remain spiritual. Your actions should be quietness, prayerfulness, and love. (I wrote these words many years ago on the fly-leaf of my Bible and have reviewed them often and shared them with countless pastors through the years.)

- "In any situation where Satan dominates and threatens, God looks for a man through whom He may declare war on the enemy. He purposes that through that man Satan be served notice to back up, pack up, and clear out." (Arthur Matthews)

Scripture: "I have told you these things, so that in me you may have peace. In this world you will have trouble. But take heart! I have overcome the world" (John 16:33, NIV).

Prayer: Lord, keep me mindful of who is in control of life's conflicts, and help me trust You in every circumstance. Amen.

The "Storm" Principle: "Immediately Jesus made his disciples get into the boat and go on ahead of him to Bethesaida ... when evening was come, the boat was in the middle of the lake and he was alone on land. He saw the disciples straining at the oars, because the wind was against them" (Mark 6:45a, 48a, NIV).

- Second-mile leadership means that sometimes we are sent into a storm by the Lord Himself. The disciples were commanded to go into the storm against their will, and if they had refused, they would have been out of God's will.

- Second-mile leaders must always understand this very basic principle: We can be in the midst of the greatest storm of our lives and still be right in the center of God's will! You see, the storms of life are inevitable. No one lives a storm-free life. In fact, someone once said that there are three stages of our lives: We are entering a storm, enduring a storm, or emerging from a storm—in which case, we're preparing to enter another one.

- It has been my experience as a pastor, missionary, and director of missions that when annual budgets are being developed seems to always bring storms into the lives of churches and church leaders. In the book *Mastering Conflict and Controversy* by Edward G. Dobson, Speed B. Leas, and Marshall Shelly, it is noted that budget and stewardship emphasis is one of the most predictable times for conflict to arise in the church.

- Second-mile leaders must be totally dependent on Jesus to get them through and out of the storms that may come. *Jesus tries us in order to make us trust where we cannot trace.*

- The exercise of faith is required to get us through the storms that come. When Jesus says, "Get out of the boat," second-mile leaders will get up and get out, keeping their eyes on Jesus, even though the circumstances around them may be filled with wind and waves.

- Keeping our accounts current with Jesus permits us to know that Jesus is there to rescue us. He is always in sight and within arm's length. Walking with Jesus allows us to walk to Jesus when the storms swirl around us.

- Storms don't last forever. "Then he climbed into the boat with them, and the wind died down" (Mark 6:51). The storm won't last forever, because Jesus has said, "I am with you always; yes, in the midst of the storms of life!" So whatever the storm may bring, it won't last forever, although it may even cost me my life, I can still rest in this great truth: *I claim no great faith, but I enjoy great grace.*

  > Before me lies an unknown sea,
  > The past I leave behind;
  > Strong waves are foaming at the prow,
  > The sail bends to the wind.
  > Sometime, I know not when or how,
  > All things will be revealed—
  > And until then content am I
  > To sail with orders sealed.[47]

Scripture: "We do not know what to do, but our eyes are upon you" (II Chronicles 20:12b, NIV).

Prayer: Lord, I thank you that you are with me through the storms of life. Amen.

The "Flack Jacket" Principle: "For look, the wicked bend their bows, they set their arrows against the strings to shoot from the shadows at the upright in heart" (Psalm 11:2, KJV).

- Second-mile leaders are in front; they are point men, ahead of their time; they are risk-takers, always getting shot at, because they are easy targets as they stay visible—they are always on the point.

- Second-mile leaders spend a great deal of time dodging bullets, arrows, or criticism that seem to always come in their direction.

- "Untutored courage is useless in the face of educated bullets." (George S. Patton, Jr).

- "When the foundations are being destroyed what can the righteous do?" (Psalm 11:3)

- The psalmist reminds second-mile leaders that when they are being shot at and it seems that the things they stand for are being destroyed, there are some things that they can do:

1. Keep trusting in God—our part is to *trust God*, no matter what—even when being shot at (Psalm 11:2).

2. Keep focusing on the fact of God's sovereignty (Psalm 11:4): God is on His throne, omnipotent (all-powerful), omnipresent (everywhere), and omniscient (all-knowing).

3. Keep the faith—God will reward the righteous; we will see His face (Psalm 11:7).

Scripture: "No weapon forged against you will prevail, and you will refute every tongue that accuses you. This is the heritage of the servants of the Lord, and this is their vindication from me, declares the Lord" (Isaiah 54:17, NIV).

Prayer: Lord, my trust is in you completely for everything that is needed for protection and direction in my daily walk with you. Amen.

The "Bittersweet" Principle: "No one could distinguish the sound of the shouts of joy from the sound of weeping, because the people made so much noise. And the sound was heard far away" (Ezra 3:13).

- Sometimes the sweetness of victory is difficult to enjoy because of the bitterness of distractions that tend to defeat us.

- Leadership is being able to lead, even though your emotions may be bittersweet.

- "It is true … your friends don't need an explanation, and your enemies will not accept one. When we go on the defensive, we bog down and cease to move forward … the world is ready to follow the man who knows where he is going. The world moves on, and a man on the defensive cannot chart the course a moving world is to travel. It is better to go forward with a little than to sit down with a lot." (Adolph Bedsole)

- I have kept a sign in my study for many years as a reminder of Who I am to please as a second-mile leader. It reads, "You will never live life on an even keel until the praise of man does not elevate you and the criticism of man does not lower you!"

- "When you please God it doesn't matter who you displease. If you displease God it doesn't matter who you please." (Steve Brumbelow)

Scripture: "A great door for effective work has opened to me, and there are many who oppose me" (I Corinthians 16:9, NIV).

Prayer: Lord, my desire is to please you in all that I do or say. Please keep my heart focused on what you have called me to do. Amen.

The "Beracah" Principle: "And on the fourth day they assembled themselves in the valley of Berachah; for there they blessed the Lord: therefore the name of the same place was called, The valley of Berachah, unto this day" (II Chronicles 20:26, KJV). "On the fourth day they came together at the Valley of Blessing (Beracah) and blessed God (that's how it got the name, Valley of blessing). IIChronicles 20:26, The Message)

- Second-mile leaders are keenly aware that Satan will do all that he can to intervene or disrupt any revival effort that is taking place among the people of God. In the case of the revival that was taking place under the leadership of Jehoshaphat, the disruption that Satan used was a war. A vast army of the Moabites, Ammonites, and Meunites attacked God's people (II Chronicles 20:1–2).

- Second-mile leaders also know that they have two choices as to how they will react when problems arise—with panic and fear, or with prayer and faith. Under the direction of Jehoshaphat's leadership, the reaction was one of prayer and faith.

- When prayer and faith are employed in life's battles, we learn that we can praise the Lord even though the outward circumstance may appear bleak. The valley of intended defeat may become the valley of blessing.

- The Beracah principle, simply stated, is that when we employ prayer and faith in facing life's battles, then these valleys of defeat become valleys of blessings. If we employ panic and fear, then these valleys become places of defeat. Satan had intended the valley of Beracah to be their valley of death; God made it their valley of blessing.

- Satan will attempt to engineer circumstances in order to turn us against God and blame him. Satan means it for evil, but God means it for good. Anyone who has the wisdom to outsmart Satan will be able to see his most diabolical schemes transformed into the Beracah "valley of blessing."

- Second-mile leaders need to be reminded that nothing anyone can do to them can injure them unless they submit to a wrong reaction. Only a reaction can bless or burn.

- Second-mile leaders know that they cannot control what other people do to them—but by God's grace, they can control their response. Since the only thing that can harm them is something under their control, they never need to suffer damage—no matter what others may do.

Scripture: "In order that Satan might not outwit us, for we are not unaware of his schemes" (II Corinthians 2:11, NIV).

Prayer: Lord, my prayer is that I may always be able to see beyond the circumstances and trust you for victory that will result in your blessings. Amen.

The "Presumption" Principle: "The king of Israel answered, 'Tell him: One who puts on his armor should not boast like one who takes it off' " (I Kings 20:11, NIV).

- Second-mile leaders, like the king of Israel, know that their victories in life come from the Lord. They dare not boast about victory until the victory has been won. The principle of presumption is simply one of claiming victory before fighting the battle. Overconfidence has caused the defeat of many a warrior and leader.

- Samson is an example of one who was overconfident and presumptuous as to his abilities and strengths. "Then she called, 'Samson, the Philistines are upon you!' He awoke from his sleep and thought, 'I'll go out as before and shake myself free.' But he did not know that the Lord had left him" (Judges 16:20, NIV).

- Second-mile leaders never should be overconfident and prideful, thinking that whatever may come along, *they can overcome.* There is no way to gain victory over any obstacle or failure in one's own strength.

- "People are training for success when they should be training for failure. Failure is far more common than success; poverty is more prevalent than wealth; and disappointment more normal than arrival." (J. Wallace Hamilton)

- "Failure isn't so bad if it doesn't attack the heart. Success is all right if it doesn't go to the head." (Grantland Rice)

- In *A Charge to Keep,* George W. Bush wrote, "My faith frees me. Frees me to put the problem of the moment in proper perspective. Frees me to make decisions that others might not like. Frees me to try to do the right thing, even though it may not poll well. Frees me to enjoy life and not worry about what comes next."[48]

Scripture: "I can do everything through him who gives me strength" (Philippians 4:13, NIV).

Prayer: Lord, may I never be presumptuous as to my abilities; may my faith and confidence always be in you for victory. Amen.

David's Mighty Men—Leadership Principles:

(1) The "Adino" Principle: Facing the Odds "These be the names of the mighty men whom David had: The Tachmonite that sat in the seat, chief among the captains; the same was Adino the Eznite; he lifted up his spear against eight hundred, who he slew at one time" (II Samuel 23:8, KJV).

- Second-mile leaders have the courage, when challenged, to face overwhelming odds. Adino faced odds of 800 to one and was victorious (II Samuel 23:8–12). With God's strength, no odds are too great. Adino had learned from David.

- You will never do anything for God until you are willing to face the odds.

- "There are no victories at bargain prices." (General Dwight D. Eisenhower)

- "One person with a dream is equal to a force of ninety-nine who have only an interest." (John Stuart Mill)

- "Throughout history the most common, debilitating human ailment has been cold feet. A leader with cold feet is no leader."[49]

- Dr. John Geddie went to Aneityum in 1848 and worked there for God for twenty-four years. On the tablet erected to his memory, these words are inscribed:

  When he landed, in 1848, there were no Christians.
  When he left, in 1872, there were no heathen.

- "'How does he face impossible situations?' was one of John R. Mott's tests for men of leadership caliber. It was his practice to encourage leaders to deal with impossible tasks rather than with easy ones, because that would draw out their powers, teach them their dependence on others, and drive them to God. The bracing lesson is that God delights to shut people up to Himself and then, in response to their trust, display His power and grace in doing the impossible."[50]

Scripture: "For with God nothing shall be impossible" (Luke 1:37, KJV).

Prayer: Lord, please give me the courage to face the odds and accept the challenges that you place before me—today and every day. Amen.

(2) The "Eleazar" Principle: Finishing the Task "Next to him was Eleazar son of Dodai the Ahohite. As one of the three mighty men, he was with David when they taunted the Philistines gathered at Pat Dammin for battle. Then the men of Israel retreated, but he stood his ground and struck down the Philistines till his hand grew tired and froze to the sword. The Lord brought about a great victory that day. The troops returned to Eleazer, but only to strip the dead" (II Samuel 23:9–10, KJV).

- Second-mile leaders accept the challenge to finish the job or complete the assignment that God has given them.

- Eleazar didn't put the sword down until the job was finished. Retreat was not in his mind—only that he complete the task at hand. He lost himself in the cause—his hand froze to the sword. He would not let go until the last enemy had fallen.

- Second-mile leaders have lost themselves in the cause of being soldiers of the cross. There is no retreating nor quitting because of fatigue or being overwhelmed by the enemy. They are committed to completing their assignment.

- Second-mile leaders are not overly concerned about why others may have abandoned the battle. They understand the danger of a faithful worker in worrying about others who aren't doing anything. They know that God is at work in the lives of others and that their responsibility is to be faithful to Him—others are accountable to God for their own actions.

- It has been said that the world is run by tired men. Don't be a quitter; be a finisher—others returned to enjoy the spoil of Eleazer's victory.

- "The man who has absorbed the spirit of the welfare state is not of the caliber required as a leader. If he is not willing to rise earlier and stay up later than others, to work harder and study more diligently than his contemporaries, he will not greatly impress his generation. If he is unwilling to pay the price of fatigue for his leadership, it will always be mediocre."[51]

Scripture: "So we are not giving up. How could we! Even though on the outside it often looks like things are falling apart on us, on the inside, where God is making new life, not a day goes by without his unfolding grace. These hard times are small potatoes compared to the coming good times, the lavish celebration prepared for us" (II Corinthians 4:15–16, *The Message).*

Prayer: Lord, my desire is to finish the work that you have called me to do, regardless of the amount of energy that it may require. Amen.

(3) The "Pea Patch" Principle "Next to him was Shammah son of Agee the Hararite. When the Philistines banded together at a place where there was a field full of lentils, Israel's troops fled from them. But Shammah took his stand in the middle of the field. He defended it and struck the Philistines down, and the Lord brought about a great victory." (II Samuel 23:11-12, NIV)

- Second-mile leaders have accepted the challenge to fight for values and principles. They are willing to stand alone in the "pea patches" of life if necessary to defend the values and principles that they hold dear.

- Second-mile leaders understand why pea patches mattered to Shammah. He knew that if he gave up the patch, they would take the field next.

- "Historical drift is the inherent tendency of human organizations to depart over time from their original beliefs, purposes and practices, which in the Christian context results in the loss of spiritual vitality."[52]

- "Shall we modify the truth in doctrine or practice to gain more adherents? Or shall we preserve the truth in doctrine and practice and take the consequences?"[53]

- "To take a firm stand on this slippery slope, one foot must be set in biblical revelation, and the other must be pointing toward biblical relevance."[54]

- Second-mile leaders must stand for small things—the pea patches are important. They must be faithful in the small things if they expect an opportunity to defend larger issues.

- The devil is our adversary. We need to stand up to him and say, "You aren't getting my life (my family, etc.)!"

- "The secret of success in life is for a man to be ready for his time when it comes." (Benjamin Disraeli)

Scripture: "His master replied, 'Well done, good and faithful servant! You have been faithful with a few things; I will put you in charge of many things. Come and share your master's happiness'" (Matthew 25:21, NIV).

Prayer: Lord, I know how important pea patches are to you. Please help me to be ready to defend whatever pea patches you may place me in—today and every day. Amen.

(4) The "Courage" Principle: "'Oh that someone would get me a drink of water from the well near the gate of Bethlehem!' So the three mighty men broke through the Philistine lines, drew water from the well and carried it back to David. But he refused to drink it, instead he poured it out before the Lord" (II Samuel 23:15–16, NIV).

- Second-mile leaders must have the courage to face the dangers of the twenty-first century, desiring only to please their master.

- "I believe that one of the greatest encumbrances of evangelism today is that multitudes of *set free, Spirit-filled, Bible-believing* Christians are bound by an inferiority complex. They are paralyzed by the fear of man."[55]

- "The SEAL organization cannot predict what specific battles will be fought in the future, but it does prepare so that SEALs will continue to have the edge no matter what those battles are. To do so, the SEAL organization goes beyond training its corpsmen to treat future gunshot wounds and training its divers to sink terrorist ships that haven't yet been identified. It continually positions itself so that it can quickly react to future situations."[56]

- Second-mile leaders know that they must be prepared to face whatever battles may surface. They must rely on the scriptural truth of Philippians 4:13: "I can do all things through Christ who strengthens me."

- "Security is mostly superstition. It does not exist in nature, nor do the children of men as a whole experience it. Avoiding danger is no safer in the long run than outright exposure. Life is either a daring adventure or nothing." (Helen Keller)

- "Courage is resistance to fear, mastery of fear, not absence of fear." (Mark Twain)

- The principle of courage involves pleasing God with our work and our witness no matter the danger around us. "We are more than conquerors through Him who loved us" (Romans 8:37).

- The principle of pouring our lives out to please God is still in vogue. "If God be for me who can be against me!" (Romans 8:31)

Scripture: "Have I not commanded you? Be strong and courageous. Do not be terrified; do not be discouraged, for the Lord your God will be with you wherever you go" (Joshua 1:9, NIV).

Prayer: Lord, I pray for courage that will allow me to always give glory to Your name. Amen.

The "Failure" Principle: "My flesh and my heart may fail, but God is the strength of my heart and my portion forever" (Psalms 73:26, NIV).

- Second-mile leaders have learned that failing is not final. They have learned that their relationship with the Lord may well be strengthened if only they will commit to learn from Him some valuable lessons from their failures.

- "Strange as it may seem, apparent failure seems to be an instrument in God's hands in preparing His people for larger service .... Not many of us believe this theology, but a man may be greater in failure than in success. I wonder how many of us are willing to risk failure in order to have God's best."[57]

- "The distinguishing characteristic of leaders is that they use their experiences as learning tools and gain renewed motivation from their failures. Regarding Abraham Lincoln, Donald Phillips concluded: 'Everything, failures as well as successes, became stepping stones to the presidency. In this sense, Lincoln's entire life prepared him for his future executive leadership role. Leaders are not people who escape failure but people who overcome adversity. Their lives confirm the axiom: A mistake is an event, the full benefit of which has not yet been turned to your advantage.'"[58]

- "Being humble involves the willingness to be reckoned a failure in everyone's sight but God's."

- "In the game of life it's a good idea to have a few early losses, which relieves you of the pressure of trying to maintain an undefeated season." (Bill Vaughn)

- "A realist is an idealist who has gone through the fire and been purified. A skeptic is an idealist who has gone through the fire and been burned." (Warren Wiersbe)

- "The last time you failed, did you stop trying because you failed, or did you fail because you stopped trying?" (John Maxwell)

- "A person who has had a bull by the tail once has learned sixty or seventy times as much as a person who hasn't." (Mark Twain)

- "Success is going from failure to failure without loss of enthusiasm." (Winston Churchill)

- "Failure isn't so bad if it doesn't attack the heart. Success is all right if it doesn't go to the head." (Grantland Rice)

- "Defeat may serve as well as victory to shake the soul and let the glory out." (Senator Sam Ervin, Jr.)

- "The circumstances of life, the events of life, and the people around me in life do not make me the way I am, but reveal the way I am." (Sam Peeples, Jr.)

The "Berean" Principle: "Now the Bereans were of more noble character than the Thessalonians, for they received the message with great eagerness and examined the Scriptures every day to see if what Paul said was true" (Acts 17:11, NIV).

- Second-mile leaders are committed to God's Word. "Do your best to present yourself to God as one approved, a workman who does not need to be ashamed and who correctly handles the word of truth" (II Timothy 2:15, NIV).

- "The Will of *God* is found in the Word of God. The more a person grows, the more he begins to think instinctively and habitually from a divine perspective." (Howard Hendricks)

- "The best thing to do with the Bible is to know it in the head, stow it in the heart, sow it in the world, and show it in the life." (Unknown)[59]

- "The Bible is God's chart for you to steer by; to keep you from the bottom of the sea, and to show you where the harbor is, and how to reach it without running on rocks and bars." (Henry Ward Beecher)

- "The Bible has always been regarded as part of the Common Law of England." (Sir William Blackstone)

    Holy Bible, book divine,
    Precious treasure, thou art mine;
    Mine to teach me whence I came,
    Mine to teach me what I am
    ("Holy Bible, Book Divine" by John Burton)

- "Other books were given for our information; the Bible was given for our transformation." (The Defender)[60]

- People do not reject the Bible because it contradicts itself but because it contradicts them.

- "The Bible grows more beautiful as we grow in our understanding of it." (Johann Wolfgang von Goethe)

- "It is impossible to mentally or socially enslave a Bible-reading people." (Horace Greely)

- "No one graduates from Bible study until he meets the author face-to-face." (Everett T. Harris)

- "There's a big difference between the books that men make and the book that makes men." (In a Nutshell)[61]

- "Sin will keep you from this Book. This Book will keep you from sin." (Dwight L. Moody)

- "If all the neglected Bibles were dusted simultaneously, we would have a record dust storm and the sun would go into eclipse for a whole week."[62]

- "Most people are bothered by those passages in Scripture which they cannot understand; but as for me, I always noticed that the passages in Scripture which trouble me most are those which I do understand." (Mark Twain)

- "The Bible is a book of faith, and a book of doctrine, and a book of morals, and a book of religion, of especial revelation from God." (Daniel Webster)

- "Preacher, preach the Word! Give them this *lamp* to light the road, this *storehouse* for their daily food; give them this *chart* for life's rough sea, this *balm* to sooth their wounds—yes, preacher, *preach the Word!*" (Unknown)[63]

Scripture: "Your word is a lamp to my feet and a light for my path" (Psalm 119:105, NIV).

Prayer: Lord, may I never fail to handle your Word in a correct and respectful manner. Amen.

The "Bethel" Principle: "Early the next morning Jacob took the stone he had placed under his head and set it up as a pillar and poured oil on top of it. He called the place Bethel" (Genesis 28:18–19a, NIV).

- Bethel was the place where Jacob had a life-changing encounter with God. It was forever etched in his memory as the place where God had revealed to him that he had a purpose and a plan for his life. "'I am with you and will watch over you wherever you go, and I will bring you back to this land. I will not leave you until I have done what I have promised you.' When Jacob awoke from his sleep, he thought, 'Surely the Lord is in this place'" (Genesis 28:15–16a, NIV).

- Bethel was also the place where Jacob made a life-changing commitment to God. "Then Jacob made a vow, saying, 'If God will be with me and will watch over me on this journey I am taking and will give me food to eat and clothes to wear so that I return safely to my father's house, then the Lord will be my God'" (Genesis 28:20–21, NIV).

- Second-mile leaders must have "Bethel" experiences in their lives. The assurance that God has a purpose and plan for one's life gives the encouragement and tenacity to face life's discouragements and disappointments without giving up.

- The Bethel encounter became a turning point as well as a *spiritual marker* that Jacob looked back on throughout the rest of his life.

- The "Bethel" experience gave Jacob the faith and hope to endure his years in Haran, to bring him back to Bethel, and then into the final phase of his life after he crossed Jordan to meet Esau and start over again.

- Second-mile leaders must not only have a Bethel experience where there is a clear acknowledgment on their part of who God is and that He has a plan for them—they must also make a commitment to God that they will accept His plan and purpose for their lives.

- Even though Jacob had received a promise from God—even though he had made a commitment to God—he is known to have reverted to his old ways of deception and attempting to manage and manipulate things in his life to go the way he thought they should go rather than placing his trust in God to work out his perfect will for him.

- Second-mile leaders must be aware that they have a choice in how they live and minister. They will either live and minister in the flesh or by faith. Jacob's confidence caused him to revert back to his scheming rather than be in submission to the guiding hand of God.

Scripture: "When they saw the courage of Peter and John and realized they were unschooled, ordinary men, they were astonished and they took note that these men had been with Jesus" (Acts 3:13, NIV).

Prayer: Lord, my prayer is that my Bethel experience may be so evident that people will take note that I have been with Jesus. Amen.

The "Haran" Principle: "Then Jacob continued on his journey and came to the land of the eastern peoples …. Jacob asked the shepherds, 'My brothers, where are you from?' 'We're from Haran,' they replied" (Genesis 29:1, 4, NIV).

- Second-mile leaders put down spiritual markers whenever and wherever they have a life-changing encounter with God, as Jacob did. They rely on these encounters to give them the courage and commitment to spend whatever time is necessary in the "Harans" of their lives.

- Jacob learned that being where God wanted him to be would not only bring blessings, but also discouragement.

- Second-mile leaders know that being in the place of God's choice for them will not immunize them from the problems and perplexities of life.

- Each stage of life had its challenges for Jacob. Events took place that demanded changes and/or turning points.

- The years in Haran were years of growth and development for Jacob. He faced deception from those he thought he could trust. Life was hard. Yet he was determined to be all that he could be in his circumstances. He began his family and built an estate of great value—however, in the end, he had to flee for his life.

- The Haran principle, simply stated, is that as a leader, you will face times of being deceived, doubted, and discouraged—even though you may be where you know God wants you to be. You must never doubt the providence of God and trust that He will keep you in His care and give you His grace through it all. You must accept the fact that God is at work in your life, even while you are in Haran.

- Second-mile leaders must learn—as Jacob did—that even though failures may come, God is not finished with His work in you.

God is working in you to get you to the place where He can work through you.

- Jacob had put down a spiritual marker at Bethel when fleeing from his brother Esau on his way to Haran. The Bethel experience gave him the faith and hope to endure his years in Haran as well as to bring him back to Bethel and then into the final phase of his life after he crossed Jordan to meet Esau and start over again.

Scripture: "Being confident of this, that he who began a good work in you will carry it on to completion until the day of Christ Jesus" (Philippians 1:6, NIV).

Prayer: Lord, may I always be reminded that you are in control of the circumstances that surround my life and that I can fully trust You to fulfill Your purpose for me. Amen.

The "Peniel" Principle: "It is because I saw God face to face" (Genesis 32:30).

- The Peniel principle simply means that there comes a time in second-mile leaders' lives that they must have a face-to-face meeting with God. This meeting will mark a change in their lives and ministries that will be forever embedded in their hearts as the time and place of their "Peniel."

- The circumstance that drove Jacob to his life-transforming encounter was the dreaded meeting with his estranged, angry brother, Esau. Everything was at stake—including the potential loss of family and fortune.

- Life pushes us into times like these. Decisions must be made that will affect us, our families, our finances, and our future. A word from God is necessary in times like these. We need a fresh touch, a fresh encounter—one that will allow us to continue to be effective leaders.

- Jacob's life was never the same after the night spent wrestling with God at Peniel. He began a new walk with God because there Jacob had a new kind of relationship with God.

- Jacob was given a new name. Jacob the Supplanter became the Prince of God. Now the plan of God for his life would be carried out with the power of God in his life.

- Second-mile leaders must seek to cooperate with God for Him to carry out His plan for their lives, not reverting to their own cleverness or selfish ambitions, like Jacob.

- Jacob's life was marked by the limp that reminded him that his weakness was a mark of God's strength in his life. People who have met with the Lord and surrendered to Him are marked for life.

- Those who have had a "Peniel" experience are recognized as those who have *the hand of God* on them. What do people see when they look at your life?

- "If God should take His hand from my life, these lips will turn to lips of clay." (Billy Graham)

Scripture: "I also told them about the gracious hand of my God upon me" (Nehemiah 2:18a, NIV).

Prayer: Lord, my prayer is that I may never forget the Peniel experiences of my life. May my life always reflect that Your hand is upon me. Amen.

The "Jordan" Principle: "Jacob looked up and there was Esau, coming with four hundred men …. he himself went on ahead and bowed down to the ground seven times as he approached his brother" (Genesis 33:1a, 3, NIV).

- Jacob's Peniel experience gave him the courage to cross the Jordan to meet his brother and accept the consequence of his deception. He was now ready to settle things with Esau and start over with this new phase of his life.

- Second-mile leaders know that a Peniel experience is necessary if they are going to face and overcome challenges to their leadership. There are rivers that must be crossed and issues that must be settled if they are to continue to be effective leaders.

- After Jacob's meeting with Esau, he was ready to move on to the fulfilling of God's plan for his life. Things were made right with his brother, and things were made right with God.

- Second-mile leaders must keep accounts current with others as well as with God if they are to have an unbroken fellowship with God. Their effectiveness as leaders depends on keeping accounts current.

- Jacob has a genuine desire to return to Bethel. "Then come, let us go up to Bethel, where I will build an altar to God, who answered me in the day of my distress and who has been with me wherever I have gone" (Genesis 35:3, NIV).

- Jacob's return to Bethel prepared him for the final phase of his life, and that was to be spent in Egypt.

- The courage to cross the Jordan was given to Jacob because of his renewed relationship with God. The encounter with Esau was blessed by God . Jacob's desire to return to Bethel was implanted in his heart by God so that the renewed relationship might forever be established.

- Jacob placed a marker stone down at Bethel—not only so the Peniel experience could be remembered, but also so the place would be a part of his life forever.

- Second-mile leaders must have similar encounters with God and places of fond memory where they have received God's confirmation in their lives.

Scripture: "Here's what I want you to do: Find a quiet, secluded place so you won't be tempted to role-play before God. Just be there as simply and honestly as you can manage. The focus will shift from you to God, and you will begin to sense his grace" (Matthew 6:6, *The Message).*

Prayer: Lord, my prayer is that I may never forget to return to Bethel each time there is a new Jordan to cross in my life. Amen.

The "Small Things" Principle: "For who hath despised the day of small things?" (Zechariah 4:10a, KJV)

- Second-mile leaders have great respect for any assignment that comes to them from God. They know that no assignment is of small importance in the eyes of God. They know that God is in the small stuff, and that it all matters to Him.

- Second-mile leaders know that there will be a time of accountability for their handling of even the small things. "For we must all appear before the judgment seat of Christ, that each one may receive what is due him for the things done while in the body, whether good or bad" (II Corinthians 5:10, NIV).

- Each great vision must begin with a comparatively small vision, and then God can enlarge it step by step. Dr Bright challenged each of his workers to think supernaturally, pray supernaturally, plan supernaturally, and to expect great things from God.[64]

- Second-mile leaders understand that God speaks through the details of their lives. "God speaks in the language you know best ... not through your ears but through your circumstances." (Oswald Chambers)

- God never appoints or guides you to do a service or ministry without being able to endow and empower you with all you need to do His will. It doesn't matter what the size of that service or ministry is in the eyes of others.

- In the book *God Is In the Small Stuff* by Bruce Bickel and Stan Jantz, we are reminded, "Don't wait to do one great thing for God in your lifetime. Rather do many good little things for the sake of His kingdom, which in itself is a great thing."

- Second-mile leaders are *shaped* by God as they are faithful to Him in the small things. As they submit to His *shaping* in the small things, they are *sharpened* for His service in the *larger things* of His choosing for them.

Scripture: "His lord said unto him, 'Well done good and faithful servant; thou hast been faithful over a few things I will make thee ruler over many things: enter into the joy of thy lord'" (Matthew 25:23, KJV).

Prayer: Lord, my prayer is that you will help me to be faithful in the small things, realizing that nothing is small or unimportant to you. Amen.

The "Crossroads" Principle: "This is what the Lord says: 'Stand at the crossroads and look; ask for the ancient paths, ask where the good way is, and walk in it, and you will find rest for your souls'" (Jeremiah 6:23a, NIV).

- When second-mile leaders come to stand at a crossroads, they immediately will heed the words of Jeremiah the prophet: "Go stand at the crossroads and look around. Ask for directions to the old road, the tried and true road. Then take it. Discover the right route for your souls" (Jeremiah 6:16a, *The Message*).

- Leadership that is effective and lasting demands that a leader have peace in his soul. A leader with a disturbed spirit cannot lead with assurance.

- "It has been said that most people in our world are being *crucified* between two thieves: the regrets of yesterday and the worries about tomorrow." (Warren Wiersbe)

- Standing at the crossroads of the end of an old year and the beginning of a new one demands that those who are leaders take time to look back and evaluate their past, look around and assess where they are at the present, and look ahead as they plan for their future.

- "In *Alice in Wonderland*, Alice came to a fork in the road. Alice asked the Cheshire cat which way she should go. He asked where she was going. She said she didn't know, and the cat responded, 'Then it doesn't matter which way you go.' "[65]

- Second-mile leaders understand the importance of knowing where they are going and where they want to lead their churches or organizations. They cannot lead if they don't know where they are going. "The plans of the diligent lead to profit, as surely as haste leads to poverty" (Proverbs 21:5, NIV).

- Second-mile leaders are fully aware that they will have to live with the decisions that they make at any and all of the crossroads of their lives. The consequences of bad decisions come to all who choose to ignore the good ways that God has directed them to.

Scripture: "I said, 'Oh, that I had the wings of a dove! I would fly away and be at rest'" (Psalm 55:6, NIV).

Prayer: Lord, my prayer is that I may always look to You for direction when I face any crossroads. Amen.

The "Cutting Edge" Principle: "Men of Issachar, who understood the times and knew what Israel should do" (I Chronicles 12:32).

- "If we are not living our lives on the wavelength of the Great Commission, our lives are irrelevant to the destiny of history." (Robert Coleman)

- Leading with a prophetic edge means praying alone, like Elisha, that others will see the invisible—"the hills full of horses and chariots" (2 Kings 6:17). Those who have most powerfully and permanently influenced their generation have been the seers—those who have seen more and seen farther than others.

- As the Youth for Christ motto states, cutting-edge leadership must be "anchored to the Rock but geared to the times."

- A famous anthropologist said years ago, "The Western mind says, 'Don't just stand there, do something.' So we in the West are action-oriented. The Eastern mind says, 'Don't do anything; stand there.' So the Eastern mentality is more attuned to contemplation than action. The difference between East and West [is] being modified somewhat as the East becomes more action-oriented and the West sees the value of contemplation. You must prepare for effective leadership by clear thinking. And the best thinking is done in solitude (Haggai 21)."[66]

Scripture: "But know this: difficult times will come in the last days." (II Timothy 3:1, CHSB)

Prayer: Lord, I trust You to give me the insight to understand the times and the wisdom to know what to do. Amen.

"The Law of Seven" Principle: "Do not lie in wait like an outlaw against a righteous man's house, for though a righteous man falls seven times, he rises again, but the wicked are brought down by calamity (Proverbs 24:15–16, NIV).

- "O evil man, leave the upright man alone, and quit trying to cheat him out of his rights. Don't you know that this good man, though you trip him up seven times, will each time rise again. But one calamity is enough to lay you low" (Proverbs 24:15–16, TLB).

- The principle of the law of seven, simply stated, is this: You can't keep a good (righteous) person down. He or she may be knocked down, but not knocked out. A good person's faith is in the One who is never overcome—it is in the One who overcomes all adversity, even death. The chances of getting up after being knocked down are 100%. Why? Because of one's faith in the faithful One.

- Second-mile leaders are familiar with the terms "the success of seven" and "the failure of four" as they relate to the success or failure in sales presentations. Never stop with just four sales presentations; the law of averages demands that you continue to make presentations which will result in a sale.

- Second-mile leaders are knowledgeable of the book *The Seven Habits of Highly Effective People* by Stephen R. Covey. Habits are formed over a period of time that will insure effectiveness in one's life or profession.

- Second-mile leaders are committed to a life of discipline as it relates to the *Classical Christian Disciplines.*[67] These disciplines are divided into three groups of four. The inward disciplines are meditation, prayer, fasting, and study. The outward disciplines are simplicity, solitude, submission, and service. The corporate disciplines are confession, worship, guidance, and service. The habitual practice of these disciplines is reinforcement for the law of seven.

- "[At the] back of every noble life there are principles that have fashioned it." (George H. Lorimer)

- Second-mile leaders have learned that their ability to get up and continue as effective servants of the Lord depends upon their ability to wait on God while they are down. "They that wait upon the Lord shall renew their strength" (Isaiah 40:31a, KJV).

- "We must wait for God, long, meekly, in the wind and wet, in the thunder and lightning, in the cold and dark. Wait, and He will come. He never comes to those who don't wait." (Fredrick W. Faber)

Scripture: "No weapon forged against you will prevail, and you will refute every tongue that accuses you. This is the heritage of the servants of the Lord, and this is their vindication from me" (Isaiah 54:17, NIV).

Prayer: Lord, my prayer is that I may place my total trust in You and not allow those who may discourage or even trip me up to keep me down. Amen.

The "Productiveness" Principle: "Our people must learn to devote themselves to doing what is good, in order that they may provide for daily necessities and not live unproductive lives" (Titus 3:14, NIV).

- Second-mile leaders have an abiding desire that their lives be productive in all aspects. Productiveness is how they measure their lives. To be productive, one's life has to continue to grow in the knowledge of the things of God.

- Second-mile leaders have the spirit and attitude of Dr. Culbertson as he writes, "Lord, when thou seest that my work is done, let me not linger on with failing powers, a workless worker in a world of work."

- Second-mile leaders have the spirit and determination of the Apostle Paul as he expresses his commitment to productiveness in Acts 20:24 (TLB): "But life is worth nothing unless I use it for doing the work assigned to me by the Lord Jesus, the work of telling others the good news about God's mighty kindness and love."

- The Holman Christian Standard Bible translates Acts 20:24 in this manner: "But I count my life of no value to myself, so that I may finish my course and the ministry I received from the Lord Jesus, to testify to the gospel of God's grace."

- "By working faithfully eight hours a day, you may eventually get to be a boss and work twelve hours a day." (Robert Frost)

- "Do what you can, with what you have, where you are." (Theodore Roosevelt)

- "As you come to the close of another year, it is always wise to look back at how productive your life has been over the past twelve months. An end-of-year audit of your effectiveness in the areas of life that matter most may be revealing.

- As you look forward to a new year and a new start, the old saying "plan your work and work your plan" is a helpful tool in guiding you to a life of productiveness.

Scripture: "His master said to him, 'Well done, good and faithful slave! You were faithful over a few things; I will put you in charge of many things. Share your master's joy'" (Matthew 25:21, HCSB).

Prayer: Lord, my prayer is that I will be productive in every way, and that You will be pleased with all that I say or do. Amen

Section Four
The Habits of a Second-Mile Leader

The "Going to the Mountain" Principle: The Habit of a Second-Mile Leader

"Come, let us go up to the mountain of the Lord … He will teach us his ways, so that we may walk in his paths" (Micah 4:2b, NIV).

The habits of a second-mile leader begin with the development of recognized disciplines that were practiced by Jesus Himself. Jesus often used a personal retreat to be alone with His Father. These times of retreat were times of *refreshment, renewal, reconnecting, refocusing* and *relaxing*. As second-mile leaders face the challenges and stress of leadership during these exciting days, there must be time taken to seek the mind of God for wisdom and direction. The example of Jesus causes us to determine that we will practice the discipline of retreating for personal spiritual development.

There are four principles that are important to any personal retreat: the retreat principle, the reflection principle, the reality (or audit) principle, and the planning principle. These principles, when followed, will be helpful in developing the *personal retreat* discipline that hopefully will become a lifelong habit of those who desire to be known as second-mile leaders.

The "Retreat" Principle: "But Jesus often withdrew to lonely places and prayed" (Luke 5:16, NIV).

- Second-mile leaders pattern their lives and ministries after Jesus. The retreat principle is central to effective leadership.

- The retreat principle, simply stated, is your willingness to retreat or withdraw from your regular activities to spend time alone with God. A personal retreat is needed when facing major changes in your life. A major change includes a change in ministry responsibilities, challenges to your ministry, or just a time to seek God's direction for your future ministry.

- For the past thirty years, a personal retreat has been an integral part of who I am and what I have attempted to accomplish in my life and ministry. An annual retreat has long been an imperative as I have taken the time to evaluate the past year, realistically examine the present, and prayerfully plan for the future. I have done this as it relates to my personal life, my family, my ministry, and my finances.

- "In *Alice in Wonderland*, Alice came to a fork in the road. Alice asked the Cheshire cat which way she should go. He asked where she was going. She said she didn't know, and the cat responded, 'Then it doesn't matter which way you go.'"[68]

- Second-mile leaders understand the importance of knowing where they are going and where they want to lead their churches or organizations. They cannot lead if they do not know where they are going. "The plans of the diligent lead to profit, as surely as haste leads to poverty" (Proverbs 21:5, NIV).

- Jesus knew why He had come to earth and He knew where He was going, yet He took the time to refresh His life and ministry by spending time with His Father in personal retreat. Should second-mile leaders do any less? "At that time some Pharisees came to Jesus and said to leave this place and go somewhere else, Herod wants to kill you. He replied, 'Go tell that fox, I will drive out demons and heal people today and tomorrow, and on the third day I will reach my goal'" (Luke 13:31–32, NIV).

- Second-mile leaders are not reluctant to do as Hezekiah did when faced with a major challenge: "Hezekiah received the letter from the messengers and read it. Then he went into the temple of the Lord and spread it out before the Lord."(II Kings 19:14 NIV)

- A personal retreat allows us to spread everything out before the Lord. We are able to get His word as to the direction we are to go in every area of our life. Our personal life, family life, and work life—every aspect is spread out for His examination and direction.

- The old saying is true: "The hurrier I go, the behinder I get." The pressure of life tends to take us to the breaking point. Sometimes the most religious thing you can do is take a nap." Certainly, rest is a part of any retreat. We have to be still long enough for God to speak to us.

- A meaningful retreat should be divided into at least three parts: reviewing the past, realistically appraising the present, and prayerfully planning for the future.

Scripture: "Then, because so many people were coming and going that they did not even have a chance to eat, he said to them, 'Come with me by yourselves to a quiet place and get some rest'" (Mark 6:31, NIV).

Prayer: Lord, help me to spend time alone with You as I realize that without You and Your direction in my life, I am nothing and will accomplish nothing. Amen.

The "Reflection" Principle: "When he had received the drink, Jesus said, 'It is finished'" (John 19:30a). "I have glorified thee on the earth: I have finished the work which thou gavest me to do" (John 17:4, KJV).

- Jesus said, "I have finished the work which you gave me to do." How did Jesus know that He had finished the work assigned to Him by His Father? His reflection on the task given to Him allowed Him to say, "The work is done." His reference is to the complete work of reproduction. His disciples were now prepared for the day when He would finish the work of redemption (John 19:30). Looking back, He could truthfully say. "I have glorified thee on the earth."

- Second-mile leaders understand that a vital part of any personal retreat is time given to reflection. Reflection—reviewing the accomplishments or failures of the past—is an excellent way to establish where in reality you are in your leadership in the ministry where God has placed you.

- Second-mile leaders know the importance of taking the time to reflect on God's goodness and grace. David, the psalmist, spends a great deal of time just reflecting on the glory and greatness of God. A portion of time in each personal retreat needs to be spent just reflecting on God.

- Second-mile leaders don't spend their time living in the past, because they realize that there isn't any future in it. However, they learn from the past by reflecting back over their ministries. A personal retreat needs to give time to reviewing past accomplishments and failures.

- Second-mile leaders not only take a look at the recent past, but also take the time to review the spiritual markers or turning points of their lives and ministries over the years. It is always good for leaders to reflect on the ways that God has blessed them and consider the whys of those blessings. There may be a need to renew their commitment based on what they may learn from these past experiences.

Scripture: "I, the Lord, search the heart and examine the mind, to reward a man according to his conduct, according to what his deeds deserve (Jeremiah 17:10, NIV).

Prayer: Lord, help me to always glorify Your name in all that I do or say that I may be able to say, without any hesitation, I have finished the work that You have given me to do. Amen.

The "Reality" or "Audit" Principle: "Buy the truth and do not sell it; get wisdom, discipline and understanding" (Proverbs 23:23, NIV).

- Second-mile leaders understand the value of a reality check—not only for their personal relationship to the Lord, but also for all of their relationships. A personal retreat gives the opportunity for an audit of all areas of one's life. Realistically, do an evaluation of where you are in life. Take a good look at yourself, your family, and your work. Be truthful with yourself.

- Second-mile leaders must keep accounts current with God. "If we confess our sins, he is faithful and just and will forgive us our sins and purify us from all unrighteousness" (I John 1:9, NIV).

- Second-mile leaders know the importance of their families and constantly give them the care and attention needed, not neglecting to provide for their needs.

- Second-mile leaders take the time to carefully evaluate their leadership effectiveness. They are sensitive to their effectiveness—or lack of it—in their place of leadership.

- Second-mile leaders are constantly guided by what they have determined to be their life's mission or purpose. "The most important thing is that I complete my mission, the work that the Lord Jesus gave me" (Acts 20:24, NCV). Being truthful with yourself as to how your ministry is being conducted in light of your life's mission is a must if you are to accomplish God's purpose for your life.

- Second-mile leaders know the importance of a values audit. A personal retreat gives the opportunity to examine what you stand for and on what principles you have made and will make your ongoing decisions.

- "Everything can be taken from man, except the last of the human freedoms, his ability to choose his own attitude in any given set of circumstances, to choose his own way." (Victor Frank)

- "Every achievement comes from a progression of small achievements. You can eat a meal one bite at a time and read a book one page at a time. Your attitude, not your aptitude, determines your altitude." (Lewis R. Timberlake)

- "Lord, send me anywhere, only go with me, lay any burden on me, only sustain me, sever any tie but the tie that binds me to thyself." (David Livingstone)

- "When storms are on the horizon, a key aspect of leadership is learning how to interpret the warning signs, check the navigation instruments, and prepare the crew for what lies ahead. Taking time alone with God to recalibrate your spiritual compass in times of bad news is the first service a leader can provide to those who follow."[69]

Scripture: "Forgetting those things that are behind, and reaching forth unto those things which are before, I press toward the mark for the prize of the high calling of God in Christ Jesus" (Philippians 3:13b–14, KJV).

Prayer: Lord, I will always depend on You to serve as my chief auditor. Amen.

The "Planning" Principle: "The plans of the diligent lead to profit, as surely as haste leads to poverty" (Proverbs 21:5, NIV).

- Second-mile leaders not only know the value of a personal retreat as time to be alone with God to reflect on their lives and ministries and to do an audit of where they are in their lives and ministries, but they also value it as a time to look ahead and plan for the days, weeks, months, and years ahead.

- There is an old saying worth repeating: "Plan your work and work your plans." Second-mile leaders take time to plan their work, and then they are able to work their plans. Values drive your plans. The things that you value determine how you make your plans and prioritize their execution.

- Second-mile leaders take time to plan for their personal lives (spiritual growth, physical well-being, etc.), their families (each member of the family and each child), their ministries (what they desire to accomplish and how they plan to achieve their goals), and their financial future.

- Planning requires knowing how you are going to prioritize your work. "Finish your outdoor work, and get your fields ready; after that build your house" (Proverbs 24:27, NIV).

- Second-mile leaders are much more than just leaders with big dreams. A goal minus a plan minus action equals a dream—whereas a goal plus a plan plus action equals reality.

- "Hold fast to dreams, for if dreams die, life is a broken winged bird that cannot fly." (Langston Hughes)

- "Think before you act." (Aesop)

- "Every moment spent in planning saves three or four in execution." (Crawford Greenwalt, DuPont President)

- "For want of a nail the shoe is lost, for want of a shoe the horse is lost, for want of a horse the rider is lost." (George Herbert)

- "Men don't plan to fail; they fail to plan." (William J. Siegel)

- "Don't cross the bridge until you come to it, and then be sure there's a bridge." (Anonymous)

Scripture: "Which of you, intending to build a tower, sitteth not down first and counteth the cost, whether he have sufficient to finish it? (Luke 14:28, KJV)

Prayer: Lord, help me to always seek Your guidance in any planning that I may attempt to do. Amen.

The "Generations" Principle: One generation will commend your works to another; they will tell of your mighty acts. They will speak of the glorious splendor of your majesty" (Psalm 145:4–5, NIV).

- Second-mile leaders are aware that their influence is crucial—not only for the present, but also for the generations that will follow. It is their sincere desire that all who come after them will have found them faithful.

- "God is committed to working through generations, not around them. The art of Christian leadership is the challenge of blending generations into dynamic synergism as a witness to a watching and fragmented world."[70]

- "Every generation must stand on the shoulders of the previous generation and reach higher." (St. Augustine)

- "The failure of one generation to communicate effectively its faith to its children results in loss of personal experience with the living God. Out of this generational slippage comes my basic definition. *Historical drift is the inherent tendency of human organizations to depart over time from their original beliefs, purposes and practices, which in the Christian context results in the loss of spiritual vitality.*"[71]

- "The holy influence of a godly person can extend over several generations even if his or her prayers are rejected by one or two generations. Those prayers live on and may yet be answered in succeeding generations."[72]

- "Prayer is a tremendous treasure with which to endow descendants for generation after generation. David was a man of prayer. For David's sake, God blessed Israel again and again over the centuries."[73]

- A *church for all generations* should be the challenge for this generation—a church where individuals from all age groups may benefit from the experience and/or the inexperience of each other.

The "Conferring" Principle: "David conferred with each of his officers, the commanders of thousands and the commanders of hundreds" (I Chronicles 13:1, NIV).

- Second-mile leaders need never attempt to be lone rangers in their method of leadership. The necessity of developing a solid base for leadership must begin by conferring with those who are in places of influence in your organization.

- David begins where second-mile leaders begin. First, it was in his heart to bring back the ark of God. The next step in the process was to share his vision with his commanders; these were the known and designated leaders around him. They made up the inner circle of leadership.

- The progression of David's leadership vision was brought before the whole assembly of Israel. Their agreement was unanimous. The circle was widened to include the priests, Levites, and all of those who were in the territories and pasture lands.

- Inclusion is the word that describes the style of leadership employed by David in this instance. Everyone was brought into the decision-making process, and the end result was a consensus by the whole nation. The moving of the ark of God became a group project.

- "If you're riding ahead of the herd, take a look back every now and then to make sure it's still there." (Will Rogers)

- "Listening sessions" is a term being used as an attempt to get input from a larger group of individuals as to their views on the direction of an organization. A second-mile leader is a good listener. Even though you may have a vision of what you would like to accomplish, the need to confer with and listen to others before acting is the mark of a mature leader.

- "The opinion and advice of my friends I receive at all times as a proof of their friendship and [I] am thankful when they are offered." (George Washington)

- "My definition of a leader ... is a man who can persuade people to do what they don't want to do, or do what they're too lazy to do, and like it." (Harry Truman)

- The most important words in the English language:

  > 5 most important words: *I am proud of you!*
  > 4 most important words: *What is your opinion?*
  > 3 most important words: *If you please.*
  > 2 most important words: *Thank you.*
  > 1 most important word: *You.*[74]

- Second-mile leaders are committed to conferring with others before committing their organizations to moving into uncharted waters.

Scripture: "As iron sharpens iron, so does one man sharpen another" (Proverbs 27:17, NIV).

Prayer: Lord, my prayer is that I may always have an open ear and an open heart to what others are saying. Amen.

The "Conference" Principle: "He then said to the whole assembly of Israel, 'If it seems good to you and if it is the will of the Lord our God, let us send word far and wide to the rest of our brothers throughout the territories of Israel, and also to the priests and Levites who are with them in their towns and pasture lands to come and join us. Let us bring the ark of our God back to us, for we did not inquire of it during the reign of Saul'" (I Chronicles 13:2–3, NIV).

- Second-mile leaders are not afraid to widen their leadership circle to include the *whole assembly*—the church as a whole—as they cast the vision that is on their hearts for the advancement of the kingdom.

- Second-mile leaders value the input of the whole congregation on major projects that they are proposing. Whatever the "bringing back the ark" project may be, it will not happen without the involvement of the whole congregation. All people need to be brought aboard if the project is going to be a success.

- The David leadership example and style is worthy of study and application by today's leaders. The first step of leadership was the desire placed on his heart by the Lord to bring back the ark. David tested his vision by presenting it to his leadership team that was made up of those of his inner circle: "David conferred with each of his officers, the commanders of thousands and the commanders of hundreds" (I Chronicles 13:1, NIV). These leaders gave their approval. The circle was widened to include any and all who were in places of leadership. The final step was to call the whole assembly together for the approval and support of all the people.

- The team was formed to bring back the ark and equipped to carry out their work with the encouragement and support of all the people.

- Some years ago, I heard the story of two golfers who went golfing with the understanding that they would be home by noon because their wives had beauty appointments in the early afternoon. When they had not returned by noon, mid-afternoon, and then by late afternoon, their wives were livid because they had missed their beauty appointments. When one finally got home, this was his explanation: "Honey, you will just have to understand why I am late. Harry fell dead with a heart attack on the fourth hole, and from there on in, I had to hit the ball and drag Harry, hit the ball and drag Harry. That's why I am so late." The leadership lesson that we learn from this story is that many times if the church is not behind the project that we are trying to lead, it is simply like having to drag it along as we try to finish what we are trying to accomplish. This, of course, will eventually get to the best of any leader and cause them to physically or emotionally burn out and either drop out of leadership or abandon the project.

- Second-mile leaders are careful to employ the "David principles" of leadership as they discharge their leadership responsibilities.

Scripture: "And David shepherded them with integrity of heart; with skillful hands he led them" (Psalm 78:72, NIV).

Prayer: Lord, my prayer is that my life will reflect that I am a leader after the heart of God. Amen.

The "Consensus" Principle: "The whole assembly agreed to do this, because it seemed right to all the people" (I Chronicles 13:4, NIV).

- Second-mile leaders know the importance of having unity of agreement among those who they are leading. "May the God who gives endurance and encouragement give you a spirit of unity among yourselves as you follow Christ Jesus, so that with one heart and mouth you may glorify the God and Father of our Lord Jesus Christ" (Romans 15:5–6, NIV).

- Second-mile leaders are consensus-builders. When making a decision, they will take the time required to bring all parties to the table for reaching an agreement on the project they have on their hearts to present to the entire organization. "I appeal to you, brothers, in the name of our Lord Jesus Christ, that all of you agree with one another so that there may be no divisions among you and that you may be perfectly united in mind and thought" (I Corinthians 1:10, NIV).

- If the process has brought all into the decision-making arena, then all involved have a clear understanding of the reason for unanimous approval of the proposal. "Live in harmony with one another. Do not be proud, but be willing to associate with people of low position. Do not be conceited …. If it is possible as far as it depends on you, live at peace with everyone" (Romans 12:16,18, NIV).

- Second-mile leaders must be committed to being consensus-builders. Pentecost has radically changed how God relates to people. A theology of unity was born that day—Christ in me and Christ in you. All believers have the mind of Christ—this being true, we must lay our personal opinions aside and seek His mind on the issues we face in the church. It is not about what we may want in any situation—it is about what Christ wants.

- Consensus is found when the entire congregation has come together in unity to find the mind of Christ on the matter at hand. Second-mile leaders need to have the patience to lead their church to find the mind of Christ about all matters.

Scripture: "Let this mind be in you, which was also in Christ Jesus (Philippians 2:5, KJV).

Prayer: Lord, help me to be committed to consensus-building so that there may be unity in the body of Christ. Amen.

Section Five
The Pitfalls of a Second-Mile Leader

The "Pitfall" Principle: "If a man digs a pit, he will fall into it; if a man rolls a stone, it will roll back on him" (Proverbs 26:27, NIV).

- Second-mile leaders have learned that their leadership should not be based on skillful manipulation of those they lead to do what they want to be done, but rather on integrity and honesty of motive.

- The pitfall principle, simply stated, is that doing the wrong thing for the wrong reason will always result in falling into the hole that you have dug for yourself.

- Haman, in the book of Esther, is a prime example on the pitfall principle: "'A gallows seventy-five feet high stands by Haman's house. He had it made for Mordecai, who spoke up to help the king.' The King said, 'Hang him on it!' So they hanged Haman on the gallows he had prepared for Mordecai" (Esther 7:9b–10, NIV).

- The old saying is certainly true—what goes around, comes around.

- You will reap what you sow—more than you sow and later than you sow. Leadership carries with it great responsibility.

- The boomerang will return to the one who has thrown it. Leadership demands wisdom and discernment at every juncture, no matter how difficult the challenge may be.

- "Malice backfires; spite boomerangs" (Proverbs 26:27, *The Message*).

- "If you find yourself in a hole, the first thing to do is stop digging." (Will Rogers)

- "Don't throw stones at your neighbors if you have glass windows." (Benjamin Franklin)

    "Sow a thought, reap an action;
    Sow an action, reap a habit;
    Sow a habit, reap a character;
    Sow a character, reap a destiny."
    (Samuel Smiles)

- Second-mile leaders have learned to lead with their hearts (purity of motive), heads (clarity of purpose), and hands (methodology that is flexible), and always be mindful that there is never any room for any kind of pitfalls to be dug, or any kind of manipulation to be employed to get the end result that they desire.

Scripture: "Cast your bread upon the waters, for after many days you will find it again" (Ecclesiastes 11:1, NIV).

Prayer: Lord, my prayer is that in all things I may maintain integrity. Amen.

The "Hitting the Wall" Principle: "Besides everything else, I face daily the pressure of my concern for all the churches" (II Corinthians 11:28, NIV).

"Hitting the wall" is a term that is used in long-distance running. You are running at a steady pace when suddenly, you hit an invisible brick wall. All of your energy is gone; it seems that your legs have become like lead, and you are unable to catch your breath. The final outcome is that you don't finish the race.

- Hitting the wall does not only occur in running; it happens in life. We seem to be going along fine when suddenly we hit an invisible wall and can't seem to move forward. It may occur in our relationships or in our emotional, mental, or spiritual lives. It is a difficult place to be.

- "The good news is that we serve a God who breaks through these walls (II Samuel 5:20, AMP). 'The Lord has broken through my enemies before me, like the bursting out of great waters. So he called the name of that place Baal-perazim (Lord of breaking through).'" (Blake McKenzie)

- "As a leader, you cannot give what you do not have; and as a Christian who leads; if what you have is not from God and of God, what you give isn't worth getting. On the other hand, the more you grow in the depth and breadth of your relationship with him, the more of value and substance you have to give, and the more desirable and significant your leadership becomes."[75]

- Spiritual burnout is a danger for all of God's servants. "Let us not become weary in doing good, for at the proper time we will reap a harvest if do not give up" (Galatians 6:9, NIV).

Scripture: "I can do everything through him who gives me strength" (Philippians 4:13, NIV).

Prayer: Lord, my prayer is that I may continually exchange my strength for Your strength. Amen.

The "Falling on your own Sword" Principle: "So Saul took his own sword and fell on it" (I Samuel 31:4).

- What others can't do to us, we do to ourselves—we self-destruct by submitting to a wrong reaction.

- We must not fall on our own swords by allowing a root of bitterness to grow in us.

- "See to it that no one misses the grace of God, and that no bitter root grows up to cause trouble and defile many" (Hebrews 12:15).

- We must not fall on our own swords by submitting to our sinful nature. "The acts of the sinful nature are obvious: sexual immorality, impurity and debauchery; idolatry and witchcraft; hatred, discord, jealousy, fits of rage, selfish ambition, dissensions, factions and envy; drunkenness, orgies, and the like. I warn you as I did before, that those who live like this will not inherit the kingdom of God" (Galatians 5:19–21).

- Steve Farrar, is his book *Finishing Strong,* says there are three major ambushes one must avoid if they desire to finish their ministries strong:
  1. The ambush of another woman
  2. The ambush of money
  3. The ambush of a neglected family

- "Beware of no man more than yourself; we carry our worst enemies within us." (Charles Haddon Spurgeon)

- "Pride is the mother hen under which all other sins are hatched." (C. S. Lewis)

Scripture: "Teach me your way, O Lord, and I will walk in your truth; give me an undivided heart, that I may fear your name" (Psalm 86:11, NIV).

Prayer: Lord, please help me to not fall on my own sword. Amen.

The "Shibboleth-Sibboleth" Principle: "The Gileadites captured the fords of Jordan leading to Ephraim, and whenever a survivor of Ephriam said, 'Let me cross over,' the men of Gilead ask him, 'Are you an Ephraimite?' If he replied, 'No,' they said, 'All right, say "Shibboleth.' If he said 'Sibboleth,' because he could not pronounce the word correctly, they seized him and killed him at the fords of the Jordon" (Judges 12:5–6).

- Knowing what and how to say the right thing at the right time is of great importance for a second-mile leader.

- It is possible to say the right thing in the wrong way at the wrong time and lose credibility with those you are attempting to lead.

- Knowing how to say what needs to be said when it needs to be said is the trait of a second-mile leader.

- "We all stumble in many ways. If anyone is never at fault in what he says, he is a perfect man, able to keep his whole body in check" (James 3:2, NIV).

Scripture: "Instead, speaking the truth in love, we will in all things grow up into him who is the Head, that is Christ" (Ephesians 4:15, NIV).

Prayer: Lord, help me know what needs to be said when it needs to be said and to keep quiet when I need to keep quiet. Amen.

The "Saul's Armor" Principle: "Then Saul dressed David in his own tunic. He put a coat of armor on him and a bronze helmet on his head. David fastened on his sword over the tunic and tried walking around, because he was not used to them. 'I cannot go in these,' he said to Saul, 'because I am not used to them.' So he took them off" (I Samuel 17:38–39).

- Second-mile leaders know who they are in Christ and accept themselves for who they are. They know that just wearing someone else's armor will not allow them to be who they really need to be in God's army.

- Each of God's servants is uniquely gifted and equipped to do God's bidding.

- Settling down to a settled-down leadership by using primarily others' ideas and methods will result in leadership that is stagnant and listless. Others will see that you have lost your vision for leadership.

- Preaching what others have already preached is not only plagiarism; it is seen as an act of laziness on your part by those who you are attempting to lead.

- God has not called you to be someone else—He has called *you* and equipped *you* for the ministry to which you have been called.

- "After studying leaders and leadership for the past twenty years, I have discovered that surprisingly few people fail as leaders because they lack natural ability, intelligence, energy, skills, or training. More often, we fail as leaders because we try to be someone whom God did not create us to be, because we lack clarity about what leaders must do to facilitate life transformation, or because we do not have the depth of character to help people rise to a better level of existence."[76]

Scripture: "We do not dare to classify or compare ourselves with someone who commended themselves. When they measure themselves by themselves and compare themselves with themselves they are not wise" (II Corinthians 10:12, NIV).

Prayer: Lord, help me to accept who I am in you and never attempt to be someone that I am not. Amen.

The "Praise Test" Principle: "The crucible for silver and furnace for gold, but man is tested by the praise he receives" (Proverbs 27:21, NIV).

- Second-mile leaders must take great care as to how they respond to the praise they receive. "Gold and silver are tested in a red-hot furnace, but we are tested by praise" *(Proverbs 27:21 The Promise).*

The potential is that the head will swell to the point that the heart will be spoiled for the ministry to which God has assigned you.

- The human tendency is to think that you should be congratulated for the work that you are doing, forgetting that all the glory belongs to God. The most pressing question for a second-mile leader should be, "What will bring the most glory to God?" The great passion of a second-mile leader should be that God be glorified, not the person.

- "God will give no rewards for having the most opportunities but for doing most with the opportunities you have. The more opportunities God gives you, the more God will require of you (Luke 12:48). Use the opportunities you have, and God will trust you with more (Luke 19:24–26)."[77]

- "His lord said unto him, 'Well done good and faithful servant; thou hast been faithful over a few things I will make thee ruler over many things: enter into the joy of thy lord'" (Matthew 25:23, KJV).

- Second-mile leaders are content to serve the Lord where He has placed them; they are willing to sail (live and walk) under sealed orders. Their spiritual relationship with God is more important than their physical location or position. "Should you seek great things for yourself? Seek them not" (Jeremiah 45:5a, NIV).

- "Be more concerned with what you can give rather than what you can get because giving truly is the highest level of living." (John Maxwell)

- Second-mile leaders recognize that *pride* is their enemy. "Pride ... do I hate .... Everyone that is proud in heart is an abomination to the Lord .... Pride goes before destruction, and an haughty spirit before a fall. A high look and a proud heart ... is sin. Wherefore the Scripture says, God resists the proud, but giveth grace to the humble" (Proverbs 8:13, 16:18, 21:4; Mark 7:21; James 4:6).

- I have kept a sign in my study for many years as a reminder of who I am to please as a second-mile leader. It reads, "You will never live life on an even keel until … the praise of man does not elevate you … and the criticism of man does not lower you!"

Scripture: "Wherefore, let him that thinketh he standeth take heed lest he fall" (I Corinthians 10:12, KJV).

Prayer: Lord, help me to always resist the temptation to gloat in the praise of people; may I always realize that all the glory belongs to You. Amen.

The "Limelight" Principle: "He who is full loathes honey, but to the hungry even what is bitter tastes sweet" (Proverbs 27:7, NIV).

- Second-mile leaders know the importance of staying in the shadows and allowing others to have the limelight. The most important lesson they have learned is never to starve for attention. This will cause all kinds of missteps in their role as a leader. Being hungry for attention will take focus away from one's ability to walk in humility as God's servant.

- It has been said that there is no limit to what God can do for and through a person as long as that person does not touch God's glory.

- Moody preached, "The beginning of greatness is to be little, the increase of greatness is to be less, and the perfection of greatness is to be nothing."

- It has been said that one who matures emotionally moves beyond recognition and fame to making a difference in his world.

- "The deeper your humility, other things being equal, the more God can use you. Holy, total submission to God and holy humility make you great in the sight of God. Total dying to your own proud self-life, total crucifixion with Christ prepares you for God to use."[78]

- Second-mile leaders are aware that God has not called them to be in the limelight or to be considered successful by the standards of the world; rather, God has called them to be obedient. Success is His to give; obedience is ours to give. We are responsible for the depth of our ministry, and God is responsible for its breadth.

Scripture: "And seekest thou great things for thyself? Seek them not" (Jeremiah 45:5, KJV).

Prayer: My prayer, O Lord, is that I may decrease and that You may increase. Amen.

The "Selfish Ambition" Principle: "Come let us build ourselves a city, with a tower that reaches to the heavens, so that we may make a name for ourselves" (Genesis 11:4, NKJV).

- Second-mile leaders must come to the place of realizing that they are not called to make a name for themselves, but rather to make Christ's name known.

- It has been written that the process of ministry is threefold. In stage one, a minister desires to be noticed. In stage two, a minister desires to be remembered. In stage three, a minister desires to make a difference.

- "One who matures emotionally moves beyond recognition and fame to making a difference in his world." (Unknown)

- "When a man is wrapped up in himself, he makes a pretty small package." (John Ruskin)

- "The final estimate of men shows that history cares not an iota for the rank or title a man has borne, or the office he has held, but only the quality of his deeds and the character of his mind and heart." (Samuel Brengle)

- The question is asked in the book *Lead Like Jesus,* "What is your leadership ego?" The answer is given as such: for self-serving leaders, EGO means Edging God Out; for servant leaders, EGO means Exalting God Only. Those who are seeking to make a name for themselves are ego-driven by *edging God out* of their lives and leadership. Those who are committed followers of Jesus Christ have the desire to *exalt God only* by allowing Him to be their leader and they His servants.[79]

- Jeremiah warns Baruch of the danger of selfish ambition: "Seekest thou great things for thyself? Seek them not" (Jeremiah 45:5). "He is not warning against ambition *per se,* but against self-centered ambition—great things for thyself. A desire to be great is not necessarily in itself sinful. It is the motivation that determines its character. Our Lord did not discount or disparage aspiration to greatness, but He did pointedly expose and stigmatize unworthy motivation."[80]

- "Never mind where your work is. Never mind whether it is visible or not. Never mind whether your name is associated with it. You may never see the issues of your toil. You are working for eternity. If you cannot see the results here, remember that God does see, and if you are faithful now, your works will follow you. And so, do your duty and trust in God." (Alexander MacLaren)

Scripture: "For promotion and power come from nowhere on earth, but only from God. He promotes one and deposes another" (Psalm 75:6–7, TLB).

Prayer: Lord, my prayer is that You may increase and that I may decrease. Amen.

The "Monument" Principle: "Absalom had taken a pillar and erected it in the King's Valley as a monument to himself" (II Samuel 18:18a, NIV).

- Second-mile leaders shun the building of monuments dedicated to themselves. They seek to meet life's requirements according to Micah 6:8: "He has showed you O man, what is good. And what does the Lord require of you? To act justly and to love mercy and to walk humbly with your God."

- Second-mile leaders must always guard against the Dizzy Dean philosophy, which is according to a statement that is attributed to him: "If you've done it, it ain't braggin." Leaders cannot erect monuments to themselves for accomplishments that they feel they may deserve.

The following are quotes from *Uncle Ben's Quote Book:*

- Egotism is the art of seeing things in yourself that others cannot see.

- A conceited person has one good point. He doesn't talk about other people.

- Some people grow under responsibilities; others merely swell.

- Some self-made men show poor architectural skill.

- An egotist is a person who is always Me-Deep in conversation.

- You are always in the wrong key when you start singing your own praises.

- To entertain some people all you have to do is listen.

- An *egotist* is an "I" *specialist.*

  I had a little tea party,

  This afternoon at three

  Twas very small

  Three guests in all

  Just I, myself, and me.

  Myself ate all the sandwiches,

  While I drank up the tea.

  Twas also I who ate the pie,

  And passed the cake to me.[81]

- Second-mile leaders have learned the value of seeking wisdom from God and walking humbly before others. They understand that humility must come before honor. "The fear of the Lord teaches man wisdom, and humility comes before honor" (Proverbs 15:33, NIV).

- Second-mile leaders have taken on the very character of Jesus and have learned the true lesson of serving others without thought of building monuments to themselves. "And whoever wants to be first must be your slave, just as the Son of Man did not come to be served, but to serve, and to give his life as a ransom for many" (Matthew 20:27–28, NIV).

- The greatest monument that any of us could ever build to ourselves would be just to hear Jesus say when we enter into his presence, "Well done, good and faithful servant."

Scripture: "All a man's ways seem right to him, but the Lord weighs the heart" (Proverbs 21:2, NIV).

Prayer: My prayer, O Lord, is that my life may build a monument to Your faithfulness and bring glory to You alone. Amen.

The "Jethro" Shared Leadership Principle: "If you do this and God so commands, you will be able to stand the strain, and all the people will go home satisfied. Moses listened to his father-in-law and did everything he said. He chose capable men from all Israel and made them leaders of the people, officials over thousands, hundreds, fifties and tens. They served as judges for the people at all times. The difficult cases they brought to Moses, but the simple ones they decided themselves" (Exodus 18:23–26).

- Second-mile leaders understand the art of delegation. "They have the ability to recognize the special abilities and limitations of others, combined with the capacity to fit each one into the job where he will do his best. He who is successful in getting things done through others is exercising the highest type of leadership."[82]

- Dwight L. Moody once said that he would rather put a thousand men to work than do the work of a thousand men.

- God cautions us about the "I must do it all" mentality. Jethro had stumbled onto a key leadership principle: "No single individual ever, when called and gifted by God to serve as a leader, has all the resources and abilities required to satisfy the leadership needs of a group."[83]

- "The graveyards are full of indispensable men." (Charles DeGaulle)

- The Jethro principle, simply stated, is that God equips each of His leaders to do the work that He has assigned to them. At the same time, He expects them to limit themselves to their assigned tasks and not to assume more than they can adequately do. Each one must accept their own limitations and have the discernment to assign others to those areas where they are most gifted.

Scripture: "Get Mark and bring him with you, because he is helpful to me in my ministry" (II Timothy 4:11b, NIV).

Prayer: Lord, help me to see the value in sharing the load of ministry with others. Amen.

The "Amaziah" Principle: "He did what was right in the eyes of the Lord, but not wholeheartedly" (II Chronicles 25:2, NIV).

- Second-mile leadership is a description that cannot be attributed to Amaziah. His commitment is best described as being a partial commitment to the responsibility that was his.

- Amaziah was not completely committed to doing what was right. He was known as a compromiser. He allowed other gods to come into his life. He lost his effectiveness and usefulness as God's leader. He eventually lost his life. Because he did not serve the Lord wholeheartedly, he was placed on the shelf. Second-mile leaders understand the importance of being *sold out* to God alone. They serve an audience of *one*.

- Christian leadership demands our spiritual best—and more. To our best must be added God's supernatural enabling touch. We must offer our best; then we must look to God to add His holy fire. Our best is never enough. We constantly need God's extra touch. We need His fire.

- Spurgeon spoke of the need for leaders "who live only for Christ, and desire nothing but opportunities for promoting His glory, for spreading His truth, for winning by power those whom Jesus has redeemed by His precious blood …. We need red-hot, white-hot men, who glow with intense heat; whom you cannot approach without feeling that your heart is growing warmer; who burn their way in all positions straight on to the desired work; men like thunderbolts flung from Jehovah's hand, crashing through every opposing thing, till they have reached the target aimed at; men impelled by Omnipotence."

- "Every Christian leader should be an exemplar, should be a demonstration of Christ's visible standard of the Spirit-filled living. You as a leader should maintain your spiritual stature, fervency and consistency, and be so marked by the seal of God's Spirit that those you lead thank God for your leadership. They should be motivated to accept and follow your leadership wholeheartedly, and both consciously and unconsciously be drawn nearer to God under your leadership."[84]

Scripture: "For to me to live is Christ and to die is gain" (Philippians 1:21, NIV).

Prayer: Lord, my prayer is that I may serve You and You alone and never be known as an Amaziah. Amen.

The "Castaway" Principle: "But I keep under my body, and bring it into subjection: lest that by any means, when I have preached to others, I myself should be a castaway" (I Corinthians 9:27, KJV).

- Second-mile leaders are constantly aware that there is the danger of being a castaway. They understand what Charles Spurgeon meant when he said, "Beware of no man more than yourself; we carry our worst enemies within us."

- A castaway is one who knows better than God how they should run their ministries. Saul is such an example: "'When I saw that the men were scattering, and that you did not come at the set time … I thought … and I have not sought the Lord's favor …. So I felt compelled to offer the burnt sacrifice' … 'You acted foolishly,' Samuel said. 'You have not kept the command of the Lord your God, if you had He would have established your kingdom over Israel for all time …. But now your kingdom will not endure; the Lord has sought out a man after his own heart'" (I Samuel 13:11–14).

- A castaway is one who allows a root of bitterness to grow in his life and thus limit his productivity. The root of bitterness results in a fruit that is counterproductive to his relationship and leadership abilities (Hebrews 12:15).

- A second-mile leader has learned the importance of forgiveness. "If you forgive anyone, I also forgive him, And what I have forgiven, if there was anything to forgive, I have forgiven in the sight of Christ for your sake, in order that Satan might not outwit us. For we are not unaware of his schemes (II Corinthians 2:10–11, NIV).

- Just a reminder to remember: sin will take you farther than you wanted to go. Sin will keep you longer than you wanted to stay. Sin will cost you more than you wanted to pay.

- Second-mile leaders always keep their guard up, keeping themselves alert and prayerful to avoid the very real possibility of being a castaway.

Scripture: "So, if you think you are standing firm, be careful that you don't fall" (I Corinthians 10:12, NIV).

Prayer: Lord, I depend upon you to keep me pure and productive in your ministry. Amen.

The "Shimei" Principle: "As King David approached Bahurim, a man from the same clan as Saul's family came out from there. His name was Shimei son of Gera, and he cursed as he came out. He pelted David and all the king's officials with stones, though all the troops and the special guard were on David's right and left ... David ... said, "Leave him alone; let him curse, for the Lord has told him to. It may be that the Lord will see my distress and repay me with good for the cursing I am receiving today'" (II Samuel 16:5–6, 11a-12, NIV).

- Second-mile leadership requires that one have the ability to control their reactions against those who bring distractions across their lives. David was on a path of retreat from the threats of Absalom and those who had joined him in a rebellion against his leadership.

- I am reminded of the lessons in leadership that Dr. E. V. Hill shared with those attending one of his many speaking engagements. He shared that he had learned three things about leadership: don't let anyone else raise your babies, learn how to plow around the stumps, and don't ever stop to slap a yapping dog.

- The Shimei principle, simply stated, is that sometimes God puts critics in our path in order to keep us focused on what we are doing and where we are going. We must not let our critics distract us from the vision that God has given us.

- The enemies of a preacher usually concentrate their criticism on his weakest points. In a preacher's life, it is ironic that his enemies usually find that vulnerable spot quickly and concentrate their fire on that area. It is simply uncanny how a preacher's tormentors can, with such ease and accuracy, get under his skin.

- "Criticism is a very effective weapon in the hands of the devil as he seeks to break the composure of God's man who is doing things in the world. Some men can take criticism as a duck takes water, and some men take it like a goat takes rain. Criticism may make a minister injure himself more that the criticism would injure him. It may be profitable to a wise preacher, or it may be destructive to a foolish one."[lix]

- The advise of Adolph Bedsole in his book *The Pastor in Profile*[85] is very timely:

  a. *Take your time!* Time solves many problems. There is no big hurry, because an old lie made right will bring more glory to a victim than a young lie corrected.

  b. *Tell it to God.* He is much more concerned about your good name because your good name also involves His good name. This is one place where I believe God literally fights the battle for his servants.

  c. *Keep calm.* Remember Jesus! No lie could upset him! He refused to panic or to become despondent. So can you, in Him.

  d. *Ask for wisdom.* Some ask for wisdom but fail to exercise it.

  e. *Do whatever you do in the right spirit.* It may give a momentary sense of victory to see the liar lose face and swallow his words, but it may forever close the door of some human heart to you and your Savior.

- I have given the following words of counsel to many a discouraged pastor or church leader over the years. In fact, I keep a copy of this handwritten statement that I wrote in the inside cover of my Bible: "The conflict is spiritual, not carnal (II Corinthians 10:3–5). If their criticism and provocations tend to get under your skin, this should remind you that the struggle is not (skin) flesh and blood ... but spiritual. The weapons of your warfare must always remain spiritual. Your actions should be quietness, prayerfulness, and love."

- "Until you have learned to face, overcome, and utilize adversity, you are dangerously vulnerable. No spiritual victory is won and no spiritual progress is made by giving way to the flesh." (Paul Billheimer)

Peter's Leadership Principles

The "Sifting" Principle: "Simon, Simon, Satan has asked to sift you as wheat. But I have prayed for you, Simon, that your faith may not fail. And when you have turned back, strengthen your brothers" (Luke 22:31–32, NIV).

- Second-mile leaders are constantly alert to the sifting challenges of Satan. They know that they are the target of his efforts to divert, discourage, and even destroy their effectiveness as leaders.

- Leon Kilbreth expressed it well when he said, "Satan never bothers a church until it invades his territory." The same can be said of those in leadership. The more effective a leader may become, the more he will be sifted.

- Second-mile leaders know that as they are sifted, Christ is aware of their sifting and is praying for them. They accept the fact that they can do all things through Christ, who gives them the strength. His strength allows them to overcome the sifting that they encounter.

- It has been said that if a leader's work is of small importance, they can be prepared for it in a little while. When they have a great mission to fulfill, it may require a lifetime to fit them for it. Knowing this, one also knows that they will endure and overcome the many siftings of Satan that will come to them as they serve Christ.

- Second-mile leaders are receptive to the good counsel that they receive from Christ through His Word. Peter had received fair warning about the sifting from Satan that was coming. He made the mistake of being overconfident (Luke 22:33), failing to watch and pray (Matthew 26:40), following afar off (Luke 22:54), and warming by the wrong fire and being with the wrong crowd (Luke 22:55). This resulted in Peter's denial of Christ and being out of fellowship with Him.

- Second-mile Leaders have learned of the compassion and forgiveness of Christ as they may have failed the siftings of Satan. Forgiveness and restoration are just a confession away.

Scripture: "'Simon, son of John, do you love me?' Peter was hurt because Jesus asked him the third time, 'Do you love me?' He said, 'Lord, you know all things; you know that I love you.' Jesus said, 'Feed my sheep.'" (John 21:17, NIV).

Prayer: Lord, I ask that you help me through the siftings of Satan that are sure to come my way.

The "Overconfidence" Principle: "But he replied, 'Lord, I am ready to go with you to prison and to death.' Jesus answered, 'I tell you, Peter, before the rooster crows today, you will deny three times that you know me'" (Luke 22:33–34, NIV).

- Second-mile leaders know that the violation of any principle in God's Word will result in paying a heavy price.

- A principle is like an equation. If you do *a,* you can expect *b* to happen. If you don't do *a,* you can't be confident of *c.* Principles are timeless truths. They apply to everyone at all times. They are like laws of nature. They can be ignored, but not broken. The Bible is full of them. Just about every decision you make will intersect with one or more principles of God's Word.

- Peter violated an important principle of Scripture when he trusted in his own ability to follow Christ. His overconfidence was the beginning of his downfall.

- It was said of a young preacher as he came humbly from the pulpit after preaching a poor sermon, "If he had gone into the pulpit like he came out, he would have come out like he went in." "The king of Israel answered, 'Tell him, one who puts on his armor should not boast like one who takes it off'" (I Kings 20:11, NIV).

- Second-mile leaders have learned that they can have no confidence in their abilities (the flesh); their confidence is in the God who has called them and will keep them if they are willing to be vigilant in keeping the principles of God's Word as a constant source of their confidence.

- "God walks with the humble; he reveals himself to the lowly; he gives understanding to the little ones; he discloses his measures to pure minds, but hides his grace from the curious and proud." (Thomas à Kempis)

Scripture: "So, if you think that you are standing firm, be careful that you don't fall!" (I Corinthians 10:12, NIV).

Prayer: Lord, my prayer is that I may always place my confidence in You and not have overconfidence in myself. Amen.

The "Failing to Watch and Pray" Principle: "When He rose from prayer and went back to the disciples, He found them asleep, exhausted from sorrow. 'Why are you sleeping?' He asked them. 'Get up and pray so that you will not fall into temptation'" (Luke 22:45–46, NIV).

- Peter is warned about his failure to watch and to pray. Jesus had said to him, "Watch and pray so that you will not fall into temptation. The spirit is willing, but the body is weak" (Matthew 26:40).

- Second-mile leaders agree with the statement that is attributed to D. L. Moody when he says, "The Bible will keep you away from sin, or sin will keep you away from the Bible."

- Failing to watch or be alert to the siftings of Satan are just as dangerous today as it was in the days when Christ was here on the earth. "Be self-controlled and alert. Your enemy the devil prowls around like a roaring lion looking for someone to devour" (I Peter 5:8, NIV).

- The age-old illustration of the frog in the kettle is something that second-mile leaders must always avoid. If you place a frog in a kettle of boiling water, it will jump out quickly; the shock of the hot water will cause it to get out of it as rapidly as possible. However, if you place a frog in a kettle full of room temperature water and slowly increase the temperature of the water until it is boiling, the frog will stay in the water until it boils to death. There is a danger of failing to stay alert to the tricks of Satan and being lulled into the trap that he so skillfully sets. "In order that Satan might not outwit us. For we are not unaware of his schemes" (II Corinthians 2:11, NIV).

- Second-mile leaders know that prayer will keep them alert and in tune with the plan of God for their lives. Failure to pray is indeed a grave danger that we are warned against in God's Word. "As for me, be it far from me that I should sin against the Lord by failing to pray for you" (I Samuel 12:23, NIV).

- Second-mile leaders are aware that there is no easier sin to commit than the sin of prayerlessness. It is a sin against yourself, a sin against others, and a sin against God. Samuel recognized that prayerlessness is sin—and that it is sin without excuse. There is no reason why God's children should be prayerless.

- "A child of God can grieve Jesus in no worse way than to neglect prayer … many neglect prayer to such an extent that their spiritual life gradually dies out." (O. Hallesby)

- Second-mile leaders know that carelessness about prayer is an indication that they are careless about other spiritual things. They are rarely ready to be used by God. Prayerlessness means unavailability to God . Peter failed the Lord in the time of crisis because he had failed to watch and to pray.

- Second-mile leaders are *prayer warriors;* they know that the slide into sin begins at the place of prayer. Failing to pray indicates a failure to watch, and a failure to watch means that they will begin to follow Christ at a distance—and following Christ at a distance means that they will soon be warming by the wrong fire and running with the wrong crowd, which means that a danger of denial of Christ is just a step away.

Scripture: "Submit yourselves, then, to God. Resist the devil, and he will flee from you" (James 4:7, NIV).

Prayer: Lord, my prayer is that I may not sin against You by failing to watch and pray. Amen.

The "Following at a Distance" Principle: "Then seizing him, they led him away and took him into the house of the high priest. Peter followed at a distance" (Luke 22:54, NIV).

- Second-mile leaders are committed to following Christ heart-to-heart, head-to-head, hand-in-hand, and habit-to-habit. In other words, they are committed to having the heart of Christ and the mind of Christ, being in the yoke with Christ, and to modeling their lives after the lifestyle of Christ.

- Following Christ at a distance is unacceptable behavior. Commitment to Christ is constant and continuous. Lack of commitment or non-commitment are traits of this present generation. Following at a distance means that there is a reluctance to become involved.

- Second-mile leaders are those who are completely sold out to Christ. Second-mile leadership is much more than just lip service; it is a total commitment of one's life to Christ. Peter, in his overconfidence, depended on his own strength to follow Christ, even to his death—yet failed miserably.

- "You are not called upon to commit yourself to a need, or a task, or to a field. You are called upon to commit yourself to God! It is He, then, who takes care of the consequences and commits you where He wants you. He is the Lord of the harvest! He is the Head of the body, and He is gloriously competent to assume His own responsibilities! Man is not indispensable to God. God is indispensable to man!"[86]

- "God's answer to a world of indifference, materialism, coldness, and mockery is burning Christian hearts in pulpits, in pews, in Sunday Schools, in Bible Institutes, and in Christian colleges and seminaries." (Dr. George W. Peters)

- "Preaching is theology coming through a man who is on fire .... I say again that a man who can speak about these things dispassionately has no right whatsoever to be in a pulpit; and should never be allowed to enter one. What is the chief end of preaching? I like to think it is this. It is to give men and women a sense of God and His presence." (Dr. Martin Loyd-Jones)

- Following Jesus at a distance means that the fire and the passion of serving Christ has been lost. Following Christ at a distance means that we will get out of step with Him. Getting out of step with Christ will lead us farther away from Him and moving in the direction of the wrong crowd, where we will try to be comfortable by warming ourselves at the fires of the world.

Scripture: "Come near to God and he will come near to you" (James 4:8a, NIV).

Prayer: Lord, my prayer is that I may always be conscious of Your presence and never allow myself to be satisfied with following You at a distance. Amen.

The "Warming by the Wrong Fire" Principle: "But when they had kindled a fire in the middle of the courtyard and had sat down together, Peter sat down with them" (Luke 22:55, NIV).

- Second-mile leaders know the danger for a follower of Christ in taking their place among Christ's enemies without letting it be known who they are.

- Warming himself by the wrong fire meant that Peter was with the wrong crowd. An attempt to be politically correct to the neglect of being theologically correct will place you among the enemies of Christ and put you in a position where the denial of Christ will be very tempting.

- Second-mile leaders know that they are different from those of the world. Peter made the mistake of trying to blend in with the crowd. He sat down among them.

- Second-mile leaders avoid warming themselves by the fires of this world. They live lives that radiate their commitment to Christ. They avoid any appearance of evil.

- "Give me one hundred preachers who fear nothing but sin and desire nothing but God, and I care not a straw whether they be clergymen or laymen, such alone will shake the gates of hell and set up the kingdom of heaven on earth." (John Wesley)

- When William Booth, founder of the Salvation Army, was asked by the King of England what the ruling force of his life was, he replied, "Sir, some men's passion is for gold and some men's passion is for fame, but my passion is for souls."

- The people you spend time with will influence the direction of your life. "He who walks with the wise grows wise, but a companion of fools suffers harm" (Proverbs 13:20, NIV).

- Second-mile leaders are careful to surround themselves with people who are committed to Christ and are effective in their fields of ministry.

Scripture: "Do not be misguided: Bad company corrupts good character" (I Corinthians 15:33, NIV).

Prayer: Lord, my prayer is that I may be kept unspotted from the enticements of the world. Amen.

The "Denial" Principle: "A servant girl saw him seated there in the firelight. She looked closely at him and said, 'This man was with him.' But he denied it. 'Woman, I don't know him,' he said" (Luke 22:56–57, NIV).

- Second-mile leaders know the importance of staying in fellowship with Christ. The steps that led to Peter's denial of Christ were gradual. His overconfidence, his failure to watch and pray, his following at a distance, his getting in with the wrong crowd, and his warming at the wrong fire led to his denial of Christ.

- Why did Peter deny Christ? Was he afraid of what might happen to him? Was it just his impulsiveness? Was it his spiritual condition at the moment? It seems that Peter was not spiritually prepared to stand firm in his commitment to Christ. Second-mile leaders must be prepared to stand for Christ at any moment and be able to endure the siftings of Satan.

- "The backslider in heart shall be filled with his own ways" (Proverbs 14:14a). Peter was determined to do things his way—he knew a better way, he would never deny Christ; he would defend Him even if necessary with a sword, but he would never deny Him. His way failed, and we hear him denying on three occasions that he ever knew Christ. Doing things our way will always lead to a denial of Christ and His way. One's denial of Christ always begins in the heart.

- "Four great impelling motives move men to action: fear, hope, faith, and love—these four, but the greatest of these is fear. Fear is first in order, first in force, first in fruit. Indeed, fear is the beginning of wisdom."[87]

- Second-mile leaders have a great fear of God and are determined to keep their hearts right with Him at all times. Peter allowed his backslidden condition to dictate his denial of Christ.

- Second-mile leaders agree with Wesley Duewel when he says, "the closer your fellowship is with God, the more He shares His plans and purposes with you."

Scripture: "I have given them your word and the world has hated them, for they are not of the world any more than I am of the world. My prayer is not that you take them out of the world but that you protect them from the evil one" (John 17:14–15, NIV).

Prayer: Lord, my prayer is that my heart will stay in tune with Yours, that I may never deny You. Amen.

The "Restoration" Principle: "The Lord turned and looked straight at Peter. Then Peter remembered the word the Lord had spoken to him: 'Before the rooster crows today, you will disown me three times.' And he went outside and wept bitterly" (Luke 22:60–62, NIV).

- Second-mile leaders are sensitive to the times when Jesus looks straight at them. They know the searching look of the Holy Spirit into their hearts. They remember the words of Jesus—as did Peter. "Simon, Simon, Satan has asked to sift you as wheat. But I have prayed for you, Simon, that your faith may not fail. And when you have turned back, strengthen your brothers" (Luke 22:31–32, NIV).

- Three times Peter had denied his Lord, and three times Christ gave him the opportunity to affirm his love for him in John 21. His restoration is complete as he affirms his love and commitment to Christ. His love eventually gave him a great responsibility in Christ's kingdom—and ultimately, a cross.

- "Thank God for the men who have risked their all in obeying the word of command, and who have come habituated to the program of the impossible. They know the Shepherd's voice. They have learned how to love the Lord their God with all their mind, as well as with all their heart and soul and strength. Such men are prepared to hear God speak to them as He spoke to Hudson Taylor:

Are you prepared to perish with me, to be counted a fool and worse than a fool by your own world, your missionary world? May I deal with every shred of your reputation just as I choose, and will you be silent? Are you willing to obey in everything, every time, and everywhere?

Hudson Taylor's day of march had come. He began to walk on new missionary waters, unfathomed waters on which no man of his day had ever dared to tread. His path was unknown and untried. Seas of trouble lay before him. How deep were those waters! One who knows has said that 'only Heaven is better than to walk with Christ at midnight over moonless seas.' Hudson Taylor's whole life was an everlasting day of march. After many years of tasks impossible and seas impassable, the old warrior said again,

We believe that the time has come for doing more fully what He has commanded us, and by His grace we intend to do it, not try to do it; for we see no scriptural authority for trying. Try is a word constantly in the mouth of unbelievers. The word of the Lord in reference to His command is not 'Do your best,' but 'Do it.' We are therefore making arrangements."[88]

- Peter's restoration brought immediate obedience to Christ for all the days that were before him. Restoration and obedience go hand-in-hand. To trust and obey is the only way of enjoying fellowship and fruitfulness in the ministry that God has assigned us.

Scripture: "'Simon, son of John, do you love me?' ... He said, 'Lord you know all things; you know that I love you.' Jesus said, 'Feed my sheep'" (John 21:17b, NIV).

Prayer: Lord, keep me faithful and fruitful as I obey You in all things. Amen.

The "Excuse" Principle: "The lazy man is full of excuses" (Proverbs 22:13).

- "The person who is good at making excuses is seldom good at anything else." (Ben Franklin)

- The second-mile leader knows that he or she cannot be an excuse-maker as he or she gives leadership to the church or organization. The second-mile leader knows that where the Lord guides, the Lord provides.

- There is a saying that is often used by Brazilians: "Quando nao tem cachorro, cassa com um gato." Translated, this simply means, "When you don't have a dog, hunt with a cat." In other words, don't try to make an excuse—use what you have to accomplish your task.

- "No one's head aches when he is comforting another." (Indian proverb)

- "It was high counsel that I once heard given to a young person, 'Always do what you are afraid to do.'" (Ralph Waldo Emerson)

- "Don't make excuses—make good." (Elbert Hubbard)

- "An excuse is the skin of a reason stuffed with a lie." (Vance Havner)

- "There is no limit to what God can do for and through a person as long as that person does not touch God's glory." (Unknown)

- "The beginning of greatness is to be little, the increase of greatness is to be less, and the perfection of greatness is to be nothing." (D. L. Moody)

- Second-mile leaders take full responsibility before God for their lives, their leadership, and their loyalty to Christ. Each one is responsible to God for the execution of his or her God-given responsibilities.

- Second-mile leaders give no place to making excuses for why they have not given their best in every opportunity of leadership that God has given them. They know that all are personally responsible to God for their acceptance and execution of the opportunities that have come their way. Excuse-making is not a part of their thinking.

Scripture: "Peter seeing him saith to Jesus, 'Lord, and what shall this man do?' Jesus saith to him, 'If I will that he tarry till I come, what is that to thee? Follow thou me'" (John 21:21–22, KJV).

Prayer: Lord, help me to always remember that I am responsible to You for the work that You have given me to do—not for someone else's responsibility. Amen.

The "Extremist" Principle: "The man who fears God will avoid all extremes" (Ecclesiastes 7:18b).

- *The Message* paraphrases Ecclesiastes 7:18b as "Keep to the middle of the road. You can do this if you truly respect God." The idea is to maintain proper balance in all that you do. Extremism will either take you too far to the left or too far to the right. Improper balance in leadership will result in the alienation of those who seek sound leadership.

- Second-mile leaders understand the importance of avoiding extremism in their lives and leadership responsibilities. (One exception is their extreme commitment to Christ as Lord.)

- A healthy balance in Christian living and leadership is necessary for effective leadership.

- Extremism is unhealthy in any area of one's life. We see what happens in our world because of extremism. An example is what took place on September 11, 2001 at the World Trade Center in New York.

- Second-mile leadership requires an extreme commitment to Christ and His leadership principles. A commitment to the leadership principles of Christ will insure that you are not an extremist in the sense that the world may define an extremist.

- Jesus is our best example of a servant leader. "Jesus called them together and said, 'You know that the rulers of the Gentiles lord it over them, and their high officials exercise authority over them. Not so with you. Instead, whoever wants to be your servant, and whoever wants to be first must be your slave just as the Son of

Man did not come to be served but to serve, and to give his life as a ransom for many'" (Matthew 20:26–28, NIV).

- An often-repeated leadership principle states, "Blessed are the flexible, for they shall not get bent out of shape."

- "It is better to bend than to break." (Aesop)

- "The trouble with Archie is that he don't know how to worry without getting upset."[89]

- "Life is easier than you'd think; all that is necessary is to accept the impossible, do without the indispensable and bear the intolerable." (Kathleen Norris)

Scripture: "We are fools for Christ, but you are so wise in Christ, We are weak, but you are strong!" (I Corinthians 4:10)

Prayer: Lord, help me to be intensely spiritual, perfectly natural, and thoroughly practical.

The "Neglecting Known Duty/Responsibility" Principle: "But if you fail to do this, you will be sinning against the Lord; and you may be sure that your sin will find you out" (Numbers 32:23, NIV).

- Second-mile leaders are fully aware that there are *sins of omission* as well as *sins of commission.* Each type of sin has its own set of consequences.

- Sin finds us out. What a warning to God's people: reference is to the failure of God's people to bring others into the Land of Promise— the sin and consequence of omitting known responsibility.

- The profound principle of missions is that if we fail to go armed before the Lord to war as Israel was bidden to do, until we win the lost of our nation and bring them into their inheritance and into their possessions in Christ, then the word of warning still applies: "If ye will not do so, behold you have sinned against the Lord; and be sure your sin will find you out." (Numbers 32:23,KJV)

- "Sit down young man. You are a miserable enthusiast for proposing such a question. When God pleases to convert the heathen He will do it without your help or mine." These words were spoken to William Carey as he talked of the need of sharing the gospel with those of India.

- A missionary statesman of another generation told of seeing displayed by the Standard Oil Depot in the faraway country of China the ambitious slogan: "Get the light to every dark corner of the world." The spirit of missions is simply the spirit of obedience to the command of Jesus: "Go ye!" It is our responsibility to get the light of the gospel to every dark corner of the world.

- "True Christians everywhere profess to believe with Jonah that judgment awaits all men outside of Christ, that there are cities whose days are numbered, sinners whose cup of iniquity is fast filling, souls whose destiny will soon be sealed. Yet we sit in our little religious booths intensely interested in sermons on prophecy and the ten toes of Daniel's image, whereas a message on missionary endeavor to spare doomed myriads from judgment is uninteresting. We do next to nothing to send earth's missions the message that would bring them eternal salvation. We seem unconcerned even to deliver our own souls from blood guiltiness. Yet all the while we say we believe that *our silence will seal their fate*, so subtle and hidden *heart unbelief* can be."[90]

- Obedience is much better than disobedience. Sin will find us out—whether it be sin of commission or omission.

Scripture: "Any, then, who knows the good he ought to do and doesn't do it, sins" (James 4:17, NIV).

Prayer: Lord, help me to be sensitive to the things that I should do and should not do. Amen.

The "Little Foxes" Principle: "Catch for us the foxes, the little foxes that ruin the vineyards, our vineyards that are in bloom" (Song of Songs 2:15, NIV).

- Second-mile leaders must constantly keep their focus on those things that are the most important, or else the "little foxes" will cause such a distraction that they will become so involved with the side issues, that their main task will lose its effectiveness.

- "It is not the devil but the 'little foxes' that spoil the vines; the little annoyances, the little actual things that compete for our strength, and we are not able to pray, things come in between, and our hearts are troubled and our minds are disturbed by them. We have forgotten what Jesus said, 'As the Father hath sent me, even so send I you'. Our Lord never allowed anything to disturb Him out of His oneness with the Father; only one thing held him, 'Lo, I am come to do thy will, O God.'"[91]

- "When Henry M. Stanley returned from Africa and his renowned search for David Livingstone, a newsman asked him the facetious question, 'What bothered you the most while you were in Africa, the lions or the snakes?' To which Stanley wryly replied, 'Neither! It was the gnats and the mosquitoes.'"[92]

- William James affirmed that the great use of one's life is to spend it for something that will outlast it, for the value of life is computed not by its duration, but by its donation—not how long we live, but how fully and how well.

- "When Robert Murray McCheyne, the saintly young Scottish minister, lay dying at the age of twenty-nine, he turned to a friend who was sitting with him and said: 'God gave me a message to deliver and a horse to ride. Alas, I have killed the horse and now I cannot deliver the message.' There is no virtue in flogging the tired horse to death."[93]

Scripture: "Teach us to number our days aright, that we might gain a heart of wisdom" (Psalm 90:12, NIV).

Prayer: Lord, help me to not allow the little foxes to distract me from the purpose to which you have called me. Amen.

The "Failure" Principle: "My flesh and my heart may fail, but God is the strength of my heart and my portion forever" (Psalm 73:26, NIV).

- Second-mile leaders have learned that failing is not final. They have learned that their relationship with the Lord may well be strengthened if only they will commit to learn from Him some valuable lessons from their failures.

- "Strange as it may seem, apparent failure seems to be an instrument in God's hands in preparing His people for larger service .... Not many of us believe this theology, but a man may be greater in failure than in success. I wonder how many of us are willing to risk failure in order to have God's best."[94]

- "The distinguishing characteristic of leaders is that they use their experiences as learning tools and gain renewed motivation from their failures. Regarding Abraham Lincoln, Donald Phillips concluded: 'Everything, failures as well as successes, became stepping stones to the presidency. In this sense, Lincoln's entire life prepared him for his future executive leadership role.' Leaders are not people who escape failure but people who overcome adversity. Their lives confirm the axiom: 'A mistake is an event, the full benefit of which has not yet been turned to your advantage.'"[95]

- "Being humble involves the willingness to be reckoned a failure in everyone's sight but God's." (Roy M. Pearson)

- "In the game of life, it's a good idea to have a few early losses, which relieves you of the pressure of trying to maintain an undefeated season." (Bill Vaughn)

- "A realist is an idealist who has gone through the fire and been purified. A skeptic is an idealist who has gone through the fire and been burned." (Warren Wiersbe)

- "The last time you failed, did you stop trying because you failed, or did you fail because you stopped trying?" (John Maxwell)

- "A person who has had a bull by the tail once has learned sixty or seventy times as much as a person who hasn't." (Mark Twain)

- "Success is going from failure to failure without loss of enthusiasm." (Winston Churchill)

- "Failure isn't so bad if it doesn't attack the heart. Success is all right if it doesn't go to the head." (Grantland Rice)

- "Defeat may serve as well as victory to shake the soul and let the glory out." (Senator Sam Ervin, Jr.)

- "The circumstances of life, the events of life, and the people around me in life do not make me the way I am, but reveal the way I am." (Sam Peeples, Jr.)

Scripture: "Because of the Lord's great love we are not consumed, for his compassions never fail. They are new every morning. Great is your faithfulness" (Lamentations 3:22–23, NIV).

Prayer: Lord, help me to learn from my failures and to realize that you never fail me. Amen.

The "Grumbling" Principle: "They grumbled in their tents and did not obey the Lord" (Psalm 106:25, NIV).

- Second-mile leaders are not known for their grumbling or complaining—rather, they are known for their commitment of getting the job done in all kinds of conditions and circumstances.

- Grumbling is an indication of a lack of gratitude for all the blessings that God has so freely bestowed on those He has entrusted with positions of leadership.

- "Life is 10% what you make it and 90% how you take it." (Irving Berlin)

- "When I complain, I do it because it's good to get things off my chest; when you complain, I remind you that griping doesn't help anything." (Sydney Harris)

- "I had no shoes and complained until I met a man who had no feet." (Unknown)

- "Some people go through life standing at the complaint counter." (Fred Propp, Jr.)

- Be like a duck, keep calm and unruffled on the surface, but paddle like crazy underneath.

- "Assume a cheerfulness you do not feel and shortly you will feel the cheerfulness you assumed." (Chinese Proverb)

- "Two men look out through the same bars, one sees the mud, and one the stars." (Fredrick Langbridge)

- "Grouches are nearly always pinheads—small men who have never made any effort to improve their mental capacity." (Thomas Edison)

- "Growl all day and you'll feel dog tired at night." (Unknown)

- "It is easier to pull down than to build up." (Latin Proverb)

- "He has a right to criticize who has a heart to help." (Abraham Lincoln)

- "Keep your face to the sunshine and you cannot see the shadow." (Helen Keller)

- "Wrinkles should merely indicate where smiles have been." (Mark Twain)

- "Remember not only to say the right thing in the right place, but far more difficult still, to leave unsaid the wrong thing at the tempting moment." (Benjamin Franklin)

- Second-mile leaders are known by their attitudes more than their actions. Going the second mile or turning the other cheek cannot be done while grumbling about the circumstances.

Scripture: "I am not saying this because I am in need, for I have learned to be content whatever the circumstances" (Philippians 4:11, NIV).

Prayer: Lord, my prayer is that I may be able to say, as Paul said, "I have learned to be content, whatever the circumstances." Amen.

The "Undelivered Speech" Principle: "I must speak and find relief" (Job 32:20a).

- Second-mile leaders have learned when to speak and when to remain silent. They are able to control their emotions and refrain from speaking when there is nothing new to be added to the conversation.

- There are those who cannot keep silent even though they have nothing to add to the conversation.

- Self-control is a positive attribute in all areas of life, especially when it comes to saying something that is of little or no value to the decisions that are being considered.

- "A closed mouth gathers no feet." (American Proverb)

- "A closed mouth catches no flies." (French Proverb)

- "More have repented of speech than silence." (Unknown)

- "Three things matter in a speech: who says it; how he says it and what he says … and, of the three, the last matters the least." (Lord Morley)

- "Many people who have the gift of gab don't know to wrap it up." *(Lions Magazine)*

- "The difference between a successful career and a mediocre one sometimes consists of leaving about four or five things a day unsaid." (Unknown)

- "It usually takes me more than three weeks to prepare a good impromptu speech." (Mark Twain)

- "He who says nothing shows a fine command of the language."[96] (Unknown)

- "You don't have to explain something you have not said." [97](Unknown)

- "It is better to remain silent and to be thought a fool than to open your mouth and remove all doubt." (Unknown)

- Second-mile leaders have learned that it is much better to suffer from *undelivered speech* than to suffer from *ill-advised speech*.

Scripture: My dearly loved brothers, understand this: everyone must be quick to hear, slow to speak, and slow to anger" (James 1:19, HCSB).

Prayer: Lord, help me to always weigh with great caution any words that I may speak. Amen.

The "Hobab" Principle: "Now Moses said to Hobab ... 'we are setting out for the place about which the Lord said, "I will give it to you." Come with us and we will treat you well, for the Lord promised good things to Israel' .... He answered, 'No, I will not go, I am going back to my own land and my own people' .... But Moses said, 'Please do not leave us. You know where we should camp in the desert, and you can be our eyes. If you come with us, we will share with you whatever good things the Lord gives us'" (Numbers 10:29–31).

- The Hobab principle acknowledges that those in leadership need someone they can trust, someone to guide them through places they have not been before, and someone who has been down the road before them.

- Moses is described as being a *humble* man. His pride was set aside to seek the help of a man by the name of Hobab. Hobab knew the desert and its dangers. Moses was willing to trust Hobab with the security of the Israelites because he knew that Hobab would not allow them to become entangled in the dangers of the desert.

- Second-mile leadership requires being humble and being willing to admit that you don't have all the answers.

- The illustration is given of the young preacher who was filled with arrogance and pride as he entered the pulpit to bring his message. Everything seemed to come apart on him as he stumbled through his sermon. Dejected and deflated, he ended his sermon and humbly walked from the platform and sank into a nearby pew. An old preacher approached him and said, "Young man, if you had gone into the pulpit like you came out, you would have come out like you went in." In other words: stay humble and don't stumble.

- "You should ask God for humility, but never thank Him that you've attained it." (Unknown)

- "We wouldn't worry so much about what other people thought of us if we knew how seldom they did." (Unknown)

- "The beginning of greatness is to be little, the increase of greatness is to be less, and the perfection of greatness is to be nothing." (Unknown)

- Mature leadership never has a know-it-all kind of attitude. Moses is an example of leadership that needs to be mimicked.

Scripture: "Now Moses was a very humble man, more humble than anyone else on the face of the earth" (Numbers 12:3, NIV).

Prayer: Lord, may I always be willing to seek the counsel of those who have been down the road before me. Amen.

The "Boundary Stone" Principle: "Do not move an ancient boundary stone set up by your forefathers" (Proverbs 22:28).

- The consequences of removing boundary stones is clearly defined in Proverbs 23:10–11: "Do not move an ancient boundary stone or encroach on the fields of the fatherless, for their Defender is strong; he will take up their case against you."

- We are to contend for the boundary stones of the faith. "Dear friends, although I was very eager to write to you about the salvation we share, I felt I had to write and urge you to contend for the faith that was once for all entrusted to the saints" (Jude 1:3).

- Genuine boundary stones are intergenerational and are respected from generation to generation.

- There is general confusion over boundary stones that were entrusted to the saints and traditions that were not really entrusted to the saints. It is easy to stumble over church traditions that are perceived as boundary stones.

- A word of wisdom for church leaders: Don't rush to make changes without first learning all the facts of why the boundary stone or tradition has been placed where it is.

- Violations of boundary stones or traditions may cause great conflict. We must be careful not to change the rules in the middle of the game.

- Some boundary stones are well-defined, while others become evident when we stumble over them (traditions, core values) or violate them.

- Take time to think about what you would consider to be boundary stones. Name some boundary stones of the faith. Name some traditions that are generally accepted as boundary stones.

- Maybe we need to remind ourselves that methods (traditions) are many and principles (boundary stones) are few. While methods (traditions) often change, principles (boundary stones) never do.

- We must distinguish between boundary stones and traditions. We must be faithful in the defense of the boundary stones of the faith and flexible in deference to traditions that may need to change.

Scripture: "Do not move an ancient boundary stone set up by your forefathers" (Proverbs 22:28).

Prayer: Lord, help me to be able to know the difference between boundary stones and traditions of the faith. Amen.

Section Six
The Confidence of a Second-Mile Leader

The "God's Guidance" Principle: "The Lord will guide you always; he will satisfy your needs in a sun-scorched land and will strengthen your frame. You will be like a well-watered garden, like a spring whose waters never fail" (Isaiah 58:11).

- Second-mile leaders know that there are three primary sources of guidance: the Word of God as your final authority, the Holy Spirit as your indwelling counselor, and the mind of Christ. "And he who searches our hearts knows the mind of the Spirit, because the Spirit intercedes for the saints in accordance with God's will" (Romans 8:27).

- Second-mile leaders understand that there are secondary sources of guidance that include God's providence, one's own conscience, sanctified common sense and wisdom, and the counsel of others.

- F. B. Meyer writes: "When you want to know the will of God, three things will occur:
  1. The inward impulse
  2. The Word of God
  3. The trend of circumstances

God in the heart, impelling you forward; God in His book, corroborating whatever He says in the heart; and God in circumstances, which are always indicative of His will. Never start until these three agree."

- "Knowing God's will is life's greatest achievement. Finding God's will is life's greatest discovery. Doing God's will is life's greatest adventure." (Dr. George Truett)

Scripture: "Therefore, I urge you, brothers, in view of God's mercy, to offer your bodies as living sacrifices, holy and pleasing to God, this is your spiritual act of worship. Do not conform any longer to the pattern of this world, but be transformed by the renewing of your mind. Then you will be able to test and approve what God's will is—his good, pleasing and perfect will" (Romans 12:1–2, NIV).

Prayer: Lord, I trust that You will reveal Your perfect will to me in every circumstance and crossroads of life. Amen.

The "Endurance" Principle—Bloom where Planted: "If we endure we will also reign with Him" (II Timothy 2:12a, NIV).

- Do you have genuine conviction that you are where you are because God has placed you where He wants to do His work through you?

- "Put yourself completely under the influence of Jesus, so that He may think His thoughts in your mind, do His work through your hands, for you will be all-powerful with Him to strengthen you." (Mother Teresa)

- "A wise man makes more opportunities than he finds." (Francis Bacon)

- H. B. London says, "Growing a magnificent ministry in any location can be started or renewed by finding a need that breaks your heart and then breaking your back to meet that need."

- "Determine that you will stay where God has placed you until God gives you a genuine spiritual breakthrough or a clear-cut release. Unpack your bags, stop looking for greener pastures, and assume spiritual responsibility for your place of ministry ... claim the territory for God and righteousness."[98]

- Your responsibility is to be a faithful servant where you are. "His master replied, 'Well done, good and faithful servant! You have been faithful with a few things; I will put you in charge of many things. Come and share in your Master's happiness'" (Matthew 25:23). "He is faithful that calls you to work His will through you" (1 Thessalonians 5:24).

- Yesterday is a canceled check, tomorrow is a promissory note, and today is cash in hand. Spend it wisely.

- The past is history; the future is a mystery; that is why you call the present a gift. (Unknown)

Scripture: "The wilderness and the solitary place shall be glad for them; and the desert shall re*joice, and* blossom as the rose. It shall blossom abundantly" (Isaiah 35:1, 2a, KJV).

Prayer: Lord, I thank You for placing me where You have, and now I pray that Your ministry through me may blossom and bring glory to Your wonderful name. Amen.

The "Staying by the Stuff" Principle: "For who will harken unto you in this matter? But as his part is that goeth down to the battle, so shall his part be that tarrieth by the stuff, they shall part alike" (I Samuel 30:24, KJV).

- "Who shall listen to what you say? The share of the man who stayed with the supplies is to be the same as that of him who went down to the battle, all will share alike" (I Samuel 30:24, NIV).

- There is no insignificant role to play in God's army. Every role is important, and all will share equal reward.

- Our responsibility is to be faithful in whatever assignment God has given to us.

- A friend gave me a little ceramic plaque some years ago with the inscription, "It's always too soon to quit."

- "But life is worth nothing unless I use it for doing the work assigned to me by the Lord Jesus, the work of telling others the good news about God's mighty kindness and love" (Acts 20:24, TLB).

- "Lord, when thou seest that my work is done, let me not linger on with failing powers, a workless worker in a world of work." (Dr. Culbertson)

- To hear Jesus say, "Well done, good and faithful servant" will mean that I have been successful in "staying by the stuff."

Scripture: "His master replied, 'Well done, good and faithful servant! You have been faithful with a few things; I will put you in charge of many things. Come and share in your master's happiness" (Matthew 25:23).

Prayer: Lord, help me to stay by the stuff. Amen.

The "Darkness" Principle: "What I tell you in the dark, speak in the daylight; what is whispered in your ear, proclaim from the roofs" (Matthew 10:27, NIV).

- Second-mile leaders have learned that there are times when they feel that they are going through a dark time in their lives. It seems that there is no direction, even for the next step that they are to take.

- Dark times come to teach us to be patient and to wait for the direction that God will surely give. This direction will come in His time and in His way. Our responsibility is to listen to what God is saying to us and teaching us during these times of darkness.

- When in dark times, we have to learn to have a quiet and calm spirit about us so that we will be able to hear and to understand what God has to say to us.

- There are dark times that come to every second-mile leader. There may be a challenge to your leadership that causes a dark cloud to overshadow what you are trying to accomplish. When these challenges come, don't panic—find a quiet place to listen to what God is trying to teach you through this circumstance.

- Second-mile leaders have learned that valleys will come and that their vision can only be realized by how they handle the valleys of life.

- We must always remember that it does not matter what happens to us, but our reaction to what happens to us is of vital importance.

- It has been said that often a crowd does not recognize a leader until he has gone, and they build a monument for him with the stones they threw at him in life.

- "Whatever my Father sends me, be it joy or disappointment, no matter how hard it may be to bear, since I know it comes from my Father, I am going to receive it with both hands joyfully." (Jonathan Goforth)

- "In 1,000 things, it is not 999 of them which work together for good, but 999 plus one." (George Mueller)

- It is certainly true that Jesus Christ is no security against storms, but He is perfect security in storms. He has never promised you an easy passage, only a safe landing.

- "I'd rather be a could-be if I cannot be an are; because a could-be is a maybe who is reaching for a star. I'd rather be a has-been than a might-have-been, by far; for a might-have-been has never been, but a has was once an are." (Milton Berle)

The "Ur" Principle: "Terah took his son Abram, his grandson Lot son of Haran and his daughter-in-law Sarai, the wife of his son Abram and together they set out from Ur to go to Canaan" (Genesis 11:31a).

- Second-mile leaders are open to God's work in their lives; they know God will bring them to a place and they will be willing to leave Ur.

- Knowing when to walk away from any situation or ministry is a matter of great importance.

- The Ur principle means that you remove yourself physically from the situation. Knowing when to run is as important in spiritual battle as knowing when and how to fight.

- The old saying "know when to hold them and when to fold them" is a matter of perception.

- All of us have faced situations where we have asked, "God, should I go or stay?" Sometimes it is easier to walk away than to stay—yet we must discern what is the best thing to do in each situation. What is best for the church? What is best for your family? What is best for God's kingdom? Does the church need a new leader, and do you need a new challenge? The bottom line is, "Lord, what will you have me do?"

Scripture: "Flee the evil desires of youth, and pursue righteousness, faith, love and peace, along with those who call on the Lord out of a pure heart" (II Timothy 2:22).

Prayer: Lord, I pray that you may give to me the wisdom to know when to go and when to stay. Amen.

The "Ax Head" Principle: "They went to the Jordan and began to cut down trees. As one of them was cutting down a tree, the iron ax head fell into the water. 'Oh, my lord,' he cried out, 'it was borrowed!' The man of God asked, 'Where did it fall?' When he showed him the place, Elisha cut a stick and threw it there, and made the iron float. Then the man reached out his hand and took it" (II Kings 6:5–6, NIV).

- Second-mile leaders are conscious of and dependent on the fact that when doing the best with what they have in their hands, God will always provide whatever they need—even making an ax head float. The secret is to depend on God for His provision and not to attempt to improvise on our own.

- Second-mile leaders are keenly aware that there are times that God *tries* them in order to make them *trust* where they cannot *trace.* When an ax head is lost and there is no apparent way to retrieve it, trusting in God's provision is the only thing left.

- "Sometimes a Christian worker has lost his power for no other reason than neglect of the Bible. Because of this, his message is devoid of freshness and fruitfulness. The inevitable result is the giving of his own word in the wisdom, eloquence, and energy of the flesh. This, God never promises to bless."[99]

- Second-mile leaders must stay dependent on the Lord for his provision, always recognizing that within themselves they can produce nothing of eternal value.

- "The man who feeds upon God's Word will become strong; the one who neglects it will be dwarfed. Both stature and strength are gauged by the quality of spiritual food eaten and assimilated. Wherever you find a spiritual anemic, the reason is improper food."[100]

- "God never appoints or guides you to do a service without being available to endow and empower you with all you need to do His will." (Wesley Duewell)

- Second-mile leaders are committed to keeping the ax sharp through their life of devotion to the only One that can provide continued sharpness in their lives and ministries. "If the ax is dull and its edge unsharpened, more strength is needed but skill will bring success" (Ecclesiastes 10:10, NIV).

Scripture: "For nothing is impossible with God" (Luke 1:37, NIV).

Prayer: Lord, my trust is in You for the supply to every need that comes into my life. Amen.

The "Trust" Principle: "For the king trusts in the Lord; through the unfailing love of the Most High he will not be shaken" (Psalms 21:7).

- The second-mile leader understands that trust in God brings a sense of permanence and stability in all of life's dimensions; God will never leave us or forsake us.

- "God delights to shut people up to Himself and then, in response to their trust, display His power and grace in doing the impossible." (J. Oswald Sanders)

- In the evangelization of inland China, Hudson Taylor often found himself face-to-face with impossible situations. As a result of his experience, he used to say that there were three phases in most great tasks undertaken for God—impossible, *difficult,* and ***done.***

- "God never appoints or guides you to do a service without being available to endow and empower you with all you need to do His will."[101]

Scripture: "Your path led through the sea, your way through the mighty waters, though your footprints were not seen" (Psalms 77:19).

Prayer: Lord, my trust is in You and You alone to accomplish through me whatever you desire. Amen.

The "Waiting on God" Principle: "Wait on the Lord: be of good courage, and he shall strengthen thine heart, wait I say, on the Lord" (Psalm 27:14, KJV).

- Second-mile leaders have learned that waiting on God is one of the most difficult disciplines of the Christian faith. The discipline of waiting is wanting in our society. To wait for God's word and His guidance in any given matter requires a disciplined life.

- Waiting on God implies trust in the promises, provisions, and purposes of God for one's life. There are more than 7,000 promises in the Bible. God's book is a storehouse of promises. Life is full of choices; at every turn, we have to make a decision, and many times we just don't know which way to go—that is, if we don't turn to the Lord and wait for His direction.

- Waiting on God implies expectancy that God fulfill His promises, provisions, and purposes for our lives.

- Second-mile leaders have learned that failure to wait on God guarantees defeat. God will not bless what He does not originate. "They soon forgot his works; they waited not for his counsel" (Psalm 106:13, KJV).

- Second-mile leaders have learned that time is never wasted waiting on God. Victory comes by waiting for clear orders.

- These are some of the things that I have learned while waiting on God at some of the turning points of my life:

  1. Waiting on God helped to purify my faith.
  2. God became more real.
  3. God's Word became more meaningful.
  4. My walk became more dependent on Him.
  5. My communion with Him became more enjoyable.

Scripture: "But they that wait upon the Lord shall renew their strength; they shall mount up with wings as eagles; they shall run, and not be weary; and they shall walk, and not faint" (Isaiah 40:31, KJV).

Prayer: Lord, my prayer is that I may learn the discipline of waiting on You for direction in every decision that I am called on to make in life. Amen.

The "Isaac" Principle: "Some time later God tested Abraham. He said to him, 'Abraham!' 'Here am I,' he replied. Then God said, 'Take your son, your only son, Isaac, whom you love, and go to the region of Moriah. Sacrifice him there as a burnt offering on one of the mountains I will tell you about'" (Genesis 22:1–2, NIV).

- Second-mile leaders are willing to give God all of their Isaacs, knowing that their obedience to Him is the most important aspect of their relationship, fellowship, and fruitfulness in His service.

- "True surrender is indicated when man is willing to give God his Isaac." (Søren Kierkegaard)

- Second-mile leaders sometimes struggle over giving God their Isaacs. An Isaac is anything that is more important to you than God and His will.

- Abraham resolved to trust God with his Isaac, even though Isaac was his son—his pride and joy. No doubt the personal struggle of giving God everything had already been determined before the test of his faith came.

- Many times our struggle is based on personalities, sons, daughters, husbands, wives, mothers, fathers, possessions, habits, or our work. Anyone or anything could be our Isaac. God works to "crowd us to Christ," as L. E. Maxwell says. God works to bring us to the end of our rope. When He has complete control, our struggle ceases.

- I must make a confession: There was a time in my life that my *ministry became my Isaac.* God worked me over on this matter until I was willing to say and continue to remind myself that I am God's, and what He expects of me is my obedience to Him in every situation. As I knelt behind the pulpit where I was pastor on September 16, 1972, this was my prayer of commitment:

  > "Lord, I have come to the place that in everything I can say: for better or worse, for richer or poorer, missionary, evangelist, director of missions, pastor, large church or small, I have no desire for my own life, but am perfectly willing to do the will of God."

- Second-mile leaders are willing to ask God to help them identify their Isaacs. Deep down in their heart of hearts, they come to agree with God about what their Isaac is, acknowledge that God is the most precious thing in their lives, and place their Isaac on the altar of sacrifice. They are willing to give God whatever He requires.

Scripture: "And without faith it is impossible to please God, because anyone who comes to him must believe that he exists and that he rewards those who earnestly seek him" (Hebrews 11:6, NIV).

Prayer: Lord, I surrender my Isaac to you; please help me to be perfectly willing to obey You in every aspect of my life. Amen.

The "Manna" Principle: "Then the Lord said to Moses, 'I will rain down bread from heaven for you. The people are to go out each day. In this way I will test them and see whether they will follow my instructions'" (Exodus 16:4–5, NIV).

- Second-mile leaders are dependent on the manna that God provides. They are willing to trust God for all the needs in their lives and ministries. Their willingness to obey Him results in His provisions for them.

- As we come to the end of each year, we need to thank God for the manna that He has provided throughout the year. God's manna is God's unmerited provision for all the needs of our lives. His manna and His grace are always sufficient.

- Second-mile leaders have learned to live one day at a time. They draw upon God's manna for each day's strength. They understand the promise of Deuteronomy 33:25b: "As thy days, so shall thy strength be."

- Second-mile leaders are keenly aware that they live only one day at a time. As thy days, so shall thy strength be"—days, not weeks, months, or years, even though this is true. They live only one day at a time; the steps of a good person are ordered by the Lord. Their trust is in God's manna for each day.

- At the beginning of each new year, we must realize that we cannot live on the manna or blessings of the past year; we must trust God's provisions for a new day and a new year. "We cannot live on the meals we ate yesterday, and neither can we maintain a condition of spiritual health by depending upon past blessings. The blessings and mercies of God are new every morning, and we are to seek and gather them each day, in order to stay fresh and wholesome."[102]

131

Scripture: "He who has an ear, let him hear what the Spirit says to the churches. To him who overcomes, I will give some of the hidden manna" (Revelation 3:17a).

Prayer: Lord, for Your manna I am so very blessed and grateful. Thank you. Amen.

The "Caleb" Principle: "Now, therefore, give me this mountain, wherefore the Lord spake in that day" (Joshua 14:12a, KJV).

- Caleb spoke these words when he was eighty-five years old. His faith had not wavered during the forty-five years since the mountain had been promised to him by Moses.

- Caleb's desire was to never quit until he had fulfilled his vision of acquiring all that God had promised him.

- Caleb had kept his mountain-claiming faith alive in spite of all the challenges that he had faced or would face as he began to drive out the occupants of the land promised to him.

- The Caleb principle simply says to take hold of the vision that God gives you and not to turn lose until you have taken possession of it—no matter how many years it may take to receive it. You know that God will give you the strength to accomplish what you have been promised.

- The key to Caleb's determination and success is found in his personal testimony: "I have wholly followed the Lord" (Joshua 14:8b). Moses verified this testimony by saying, "because thou hast wholly followed the Lord" (Joshua 14:9b).

- "And Joshua blessed him, and gave unto Caleb, the son of Jephunneh, Hebron for an inheritance. Hebron, therefore, became the inheritance of Caleb … unto this day, because that he wholly followed the Lord God of Israel" (Joshua 14:13–14, KJV).

- The life of Caleb had been one of total commitment from beginning to end. He finished strong.

- In leadership or in life, it is not how you start that matters. It's how you finish that counts.

- The desire to *finish strong* should be the goal of every second-mile leader.

- "Lord, when thou seest that my work is done, let me not linger on with failing powers, a workless worker in a world of work." (Dr. Culberston)

- To hear Jesus say, "Well done, good and faithful servant" will mean that I have finished strong.

Scripture: "But life is worth nothing unless I use it for doing the work assigned to me by the Lord Jesus, the work of telling others the good news about God's mighty kindness and love" (Acts 20:24, TLB).

Prayer: Lord, my desire is to wholly follow You with all my heart—all the days of my life. Amen.

Principle of "Starting Over": "My friends, I don't feel that I have already arrived. But I forget what is behind, and I struggle for what is ahead. I run toward the goal, so I can win the prize of being called to heaven. This is the prize God offers because of what Christ has done" (Philippians 3:13–14, *The Promise*).

- Second-mile leaders never are satisfied living in the past, nor in thinking that they have done all that they can do. There is always another challenge—another mountain to claim.

- Second-mile leaders have the spirit of Caleb: "But because my servant Caleb has a different spirit and follows me wholeheartedly, I will bring him into the land he went to, and his descendants will inherit it" (Numbers 14:24, NIV).

- Second-mile leaders like Caleb have a mountain-claiming spirit: "Now therefore give me this mountain, whereof the Lord spake in that day; for thou heardest in that day how the Anakims were there, and that the cities were great and fenced: if so the Lord will be with me, then I shall be able to drive them out, as the Lord said" (Joshua 14:12, KJV).

- "Caleb was eighty-five years old, facing an uncertain future yet was willing to put the past behind him. At a time when the ease and comfort of retirement seemed predictable, he fearlessly faced the invisible giants of the mountain."[103]

- Starting over brings its challenges and its opportunities. There will be giants to face and walled cities to penetrate—yet this will be accomplished as we wholeheartedly follow the Lord in the new year ahead.

- Starting over requires an honest evaluation of where you are at the present and a genuine desire to get somewhere else. Jonah knew where he was—in a fish's belly. The prodigal son knew where he was—a pig pen. Admitting where you are is the first step in starting over. Knowing where you want to go or what you want to accomplish is the next step. Developing a game plan as to what you must do to get where you want to go is the next step.

- Second-mile leaders work from a pre-determined agenda—planning is a part of their lives, yet they remain flexible and sensitive to God's direction for changes He mandates at a moment's notice.

Scripture: "Forget the former things; do not dwell on the past. See, I am doing a new thing! Now it springs up; do you not perceive it? I am making a way in the desert and streams in the wasteland" (Isaiah 43:18–19, NIV).

Prayer: Lord, help me to always keep my focus on You and what You desire to do through me. Amen.

The "Wise Counsel" Principle: "Blessed is the man who does not walk in the counsel of the wicked" (Psalms 1:1a).

- The second-mile leaders do not take counsel from their fears, but rather they seek wise counsel from those who have been down the road before them. They knows that "He who walks with the wise grows wise" (Proverbs 13:20).

- A second-mile leader finds truth in the old saying, "if you always do what you've always done, then you will always get what you've always gotten."Anonymous

- "Too many people, when they make a mistake, just keep stubbornly plowing ahead and end up repeating the same mistakes. I believe in the motto, *try and try again*. But the way I read it, it says, *try, then stop and think. Then try again."* (William Dean Singleton)

- "Wisdom is the faculty of making the best use of knowledge, a combination of discernment, judgment, sagacity, and similar powers …. in Scripture, right judgment concerning spiritual and moral truth." (Webster)

- "Wisdom is nine-tenths a matter of being wise in time," said Theodore Roosevelt. "Most of us are too often wise after the event."

Scripture: "Make plans by seeking advice" (Proverbs 20:18a).

Prayer: Lord, may I have the humility and the wisdom to seek wisdom from You and from others who have gained their wisdom from walking with you. Amen.

The "Tattoo" Principle: "See, I have tattooed your name upon my palm and ever before me is a picture of Jerusalem's walls in ruins" (Isaiah 49:16, TLB).

- Second-mile leaders are confident that God has not and will not forget them as their names are not only tattooed in the palm of God's hand, but are also tucked away in His heart of hearts.

- Second-mile leaders know that God knows who they are and to whom they belong. They are encouraged by His Word that simply states, "The Lord knows those who are His" (II Timothy 2:16b, NIV).

- Second-mile leaders find great hope in the truth of Romans 14:8: "If we live, we live to the Lord; and if we die, we die to the Lord. So whether we live or die, we belong to the Lord."

- The words of the old hymn Now I Belong to Jesus by Norman J. Clayton give great encouragement:

   "Jesus, my Lord, will love me forever,
   From Him no power of evil can sever,
   He gave His life to ransom my soul,
   Now I belong to Him;

> Now I belong to Jesus, Jesus belongs to me,
> Not for the years of time alone, But for eternity."

- "God has taken the believer to be His own, and His proprietorship of the life is in itself a call and a challenge to holiness. God has redeemed us that He might possess us, and He possesses us that He may conform us to the image of His Son …. He not only desires to take possession of us, but to assume control. He is not content to be recognized only as the owner of the house, but purposes as well to be manager of the household. He is not satisfied to become something to us, but wishes to be everything."[104]

- Second-mile leaders have confidence that they have received God's "tattoo" on their lives and are committed to yielding their lives to their Master without hesitation or reservation. Yielding means that one has definitely, deliberately, voluntarily transferred the undivided possession, control, and use of his whole being, spirit, soul, and body from self to Christ, to whom it rightly belongs by creation and purchase. In yielding to Christ, we crown Him Lord of all in our lives.

- "Consecration does not confer ownership, it presumes it. It is not in order to be His, but because we are His, that we yield up our lives. It is *purchase* that gives *title; delivery* simply gives *possession.* The question is not, 'Do I belong to God?' but, 'Have I yielded to God that which already belongs to Him?'"[105]

Scripture: "Do you not know that your body is a temple of the Holy Spirit, who is in you, whom you have received from God? You are not your own; you were bought at a price. Therefore honor God with your body" (I Corinthians 6:19–20, NIV).

Prayer: Lord, help me to always remember that I belong to Jesus. Amen.

The "Resurrection" Principle: "Jesus said to her, 'I am the resurrection and the life. He who believes in me will live, even though he dies; and whoever lives and believes in me will never die. Do you believe this?'" (John 11:25–26, NIV).

- Second-mile leaders understand that the resurrection of Jesus Christ from the dead is the promise of their resurrection. They live their lives committed to and serving a living Savior, knowing that they have victory over death.

- Dr. Jose Maria, a Brazilian psychologist and university professor, tells of his coming to Christ after a long struggle when he read and affirmed his belief in the verses found in John 11:25–26.

- "Death has lost its sting and the grave its victory in the resurrection of our Savior, Jesus Christ. He could not be held within the sealed tomb of empire. Death was unable to write *finis* to his life. After the blackout of Calvary, there came the dawn and light in the garden. Since then humanity has had a more radiant hope of immortality. The risen Christ lives forevermore! And that foundation stone of the Christian gospel holds the most comforting of all promises to life: 'Because I live, ye shall live also.' That is a shining lamp in the darkness."[106]

- "There is in the heart of God, and always has been, a cross and an empty tomb." (Studdert Kennedy)

- "Martineau remarked that we do not believe in immortality because we can prove it, but we try to prove it because we cannot help believing it."[107]

- "The Third Day at Sundown" is the title of a sermon by Roy Lawson Tawes in his book, *The Global Christ*. The sermon was preached during the years of World War II. Tawes's challenge was simply to say that we should not make the mistake of reading the headlines of man but instead should read the lifelines of God. Those who walked the road to Emmaus on the day of the resurrection were about to have their eyes opened to the fact that Jesus was alive and that they had not been abandoned. They could still count on God. They were not left without hope. Christ is indeed the resurrection and the life.

- "Never was the character of God more at stake than at Calvary. He who had always seen his people through could not fail them now. The good God could not leave his loved ones with a dead Christ on their hands! That Christ must come alive again to walk on Emmaus Road. Declared Bossuet, 'Whenever Christianity has struck out a new path in her journey it has been because the personality of Jesus had once again become living, and a ray from its being had once more illumined the world.'"[108]

Scripture: "For what I received I passed on to you as of first importance: that Christ died for our sins according to the Scriptures, that he was buried, that he was raised on the third day according to the Scriptures" (I Corinthians 15:3–4, NIV).

Prayer: Lord, may I always be mindful that You indeed are alive and living in me. Amen.

Section Seven
The Agenda of a Second-Mile Leader

The "Perception" Principle: "He looked up and said, 'I see people; they look like trees walking around.' Once more Jesus put his hands on the man's eyes. Then his eyes were opened, his sight was restored and he saw everything clearly" (Mark 8:24–25, NIV).

- Second-mile leaders are aware that everyone does not see things from the same perspective. I remember very vividly a blind woman wanting to see the mission plane when we had landed in a village in Brazil. She carefully examined the small plane by feeling it with her hands from its nose to its tail, making a complete circle around the small plane. When she had completed her examination, she exclaimed, "Now I have seen an airplane." In her mind, the shape of the plane had taken form.

- Second-mile leaders understand that how they see the problem might not be how others see the problem.

- Second-mile leaders have the responsibility of making sure that they understand the perspective of those who ultimately authorize their mission. They must have and keep on their hearts what God has on His heart—a lost world. Clear vision comes only by being continuously touched by the Master's hand. Only Christ can give the true perspective.

- "The upward look of a mature Christian is not to the mountains, but to the God who made the mountains."[109]

- "The forward look is the look that sees everything in God's perspective whereby His wonderful distance is put on the things that are near."[110]

- "The surest test of maturity is the power to look back without blinking anything. When we look back we get either hopelessly despairing or hopelessly conceited. The difference between the natural backward look and the spiritual backward look is in what we forget. Forgetting in the spiritual domain is the gift of God. The Spirit of God never allows us to forget what we have been, but He does make us forget what we have attained to, which is quite unnatural."[111]

Scripture: "And thine ear shall hear thee saying, 'This is the way, walk ye in it; when ye turn to the right hand, and when ye turn to the left' " (Isaiah 30:21, KJV).

Prayer: Lord, my prayer is that You may touch my spiritual eyes so that my perception will be yours. Amen.

The "Proper Discernment" Principle: "Wisdom reposes in the heart of the discerning and even among fools she lets herself be known" (Proverbs 14:33, NIV).

- Second-mile leaders are constantly concerned with how they are able to discern matters that affect their leadership. They may feel assured that they are leading their church or organization in the proper direction, yet they are concerned about discerning the proper timing as to when and how they are to move in that direction.

- "Some people get into trouble because they focus their attention on things beyond their control. Fred Smith, leadership expert, says, 'The key to positive action is to know the difference between a problem and a fact. A problem is something that can be solved. A fact of life is something that must be accepted.'"[112]

- "Most people would rush ahead and implement a solution before they know what the problem is." (Q.T. Wiles)

- "Define the problem before you pursue a solution." (John Williams)

- "People would rather live with a problem they cannot solve than accept a solution they cannot understand." (Robert Woolsey)

- "Asking the right questions takes as much skill as giving the right answers." (Robert Half)

- "Be selective. Keep your mind available for critical information on which you will be required to act." (Rosemary McMahon)

- Second-mile leaders are constantly seeking to have good judgment and proper discernment as they exercise wise leadership. "My son preserve sound judgment and discernment, do not let them out of your sight" (Proverbs 3:2, NIV).

- Second-mile leaders receive words of rebuke and become better leaders because of what they learn from them. "A rebuke impresses a man of discernment more than a hundred lashes a fool" (Proverbs 17:1, NIV).

- "A rich man may be wise in his own eyes, but a poor man who has discernment sees through him" (Proverbs 28:11, NIV).

Scripture: "I am your servant; give me discernment that I may understand your statutes" (Psalm 119:125, NIV).

Prayer: Lord, my prayer is that You will give to me the ability to discern right from wrong, the good from the bad—and that I will know when to speak and when to be silent. Amen.

The "Focus" Principle: "For my determined purpose is that I may know Him; that I may progressively become more deeply and intimately acquainted with Him, perceiving and recognizing and understanding the wonders of His Person more strongly and more clearly. And that I may in the same way come to know the power overflowing from His resurrection which it exerts over believers; and that I may share His sufferings as to be continually transformed in spirit into His likeness even to His death" (Philippians 3:10, AMP).

- Living a disciplined life means having the ability to keep focus on life's priorities. It is easy to lose focus.

- "If you chase two rabbits, both will escape." (Ancient Proverb)

- Only those who see the invisible can do the impossible.

- One's worth may not depend on what one can do, but on how much one can take and still keep going.

- My personal mission statement is to know Christ and to make Christ known.

Scripture: "Yet I hold this against you: You have forsaken your first love" (Revelation 2:4).

Prayer: Lord, my prayer is that I may know You more deeply and make You known more effectively. Amen.

The "Priority" Principle: "Finish your outdoor work and get your fields ready; after that build your house" (Proverbs 24:27).

- Second-mile leaders have predetermined priorities and are committed to keeping them in focus at all times.

- Prioritize your plans and work toward implementing your plans according to your priorities.

- "Procrastination, the thief of time, is one of the devil's most potent weapons in defrauding man of his eternal heritage. It is a habit that is absolutely fatal to effective leadership. Its subtlety and power lie in the fact that it corresponds so well to our natural inclinations and innate reluctance to make important decisions. Making decisions and carrying them through always involves considerable moral effort. But instead of making that effort easier, the passage of time has the reverse effect. The decision will be even more difficult to make tomorrow. 'Do it now' is a principle of action which has led many a man to worldly success, and it is no less relevant in the realm of the spiritual."[113]

- It has been my practice to make a list every day, and when I finish something on my list I cross it out. I feel very good when I see the list all crossed out. I look at my list of things to do and I can plan my time realistically.

Scripture: "Be very careful, then, how you live; not as unwise but as wise, making the most of every opportunity, because the days are evil" (Ephesians 5:15–16).

Prayer: Lord, my prayer is that Your priorities will always be mine; help me to be very wise in how I use my time. Amen.

The "20/20 Hindsight" Principle: "To the law and to the testimony: if they speak not according to this word, it is because there is no light in them" (Isaiah 8:20, KJV).

- Second-mile leaders learn from their mistakes and have very clear 20/20 vision as they look back over the violation of any biblical principle.

- Second-mile leaders know that when biblical principles are violated, there is a consequence to be paid.

- Most Christians are promise-centered—we are looking for something else God must do for us. When it comes to decision-making, *principles* are far more helpful than *promises*.

- Principles are timeless truths. They apply to everyone at all times. They are like laws of nature. They can be ignored, but not broken. The Bible is full of them. Just about every decision you make will intersect with one or more principles from God's Word. Some examples:

  "We always reap what we sow" (Galatians 6:7).

  "The people you spend time with will influence the direction of your life" (Proverbs13:20).

  "The person who hates to be corrected will eventually make stupid mistakes" (Proverbs 12:1).

  "Liars are always found out" (Proverbs 12:19).

  "What you hold on to will diminish, but what you give will be multiplied" (II Corinthians 9:6).

  "God always provides for [supplies] the needs of the generous" (Philippians 4:19).

- Second-mile leaders have determined in advance that they will not knowingly violate any of God's principles.

- Second-mile leaders understand that patterns spring from principles. God is always working according to His principles, patterns, and purposes for us. When there is a violation of His principles, we are liable to pay the consequences of our disobedience.

Scripture: "Who may ascend the hill of the Lord? Who may stand in his holy place? He who has clean hands and a pure heart, who does not lift his soul to an idol or swear by what is false" (Psalm 24:3–4, NIV).

Prayer: Lord, my prayer is that I will never—in any fashion—violate any principle of Your Word. Amen.

The "Times" Principle: "But I trust in you, O Lord; I say, 'You are my God.' My times are in your hands" (Psalm 31:14–15a, NIV).

- Second-mile leaders have a clear understanding that their times, or lives, are in the hands of God. This is a fact that is readily acknowledged, believed, received, and walked in, lived in, and experienced to the utmost by every child of God.

- Second-mile leaders have taken God at His word by faith and trust Him with whatever the circumstance may be or appear to be. Faith asks us to obey and to move forward under sealed orders. Without obedience to the requirements of faith, the light dies, and faith grows dim.

- Second-mile leaders do not have to plan their lives; they seek God's plans for their lives. God has a plan for each of us. God's plan is His will. His will is in His hands, and that means that their times must unfold His will.

- Second-mile leaders understand that their times include the little things. Minutes as well as days are in God's times for each of us. Our daily routine and the people that come across our paths are all part of God's plan.

- Second-mile leaders are aware that health and strength are in His times. (Jehovah Rapha, Jehovah Healer) Exodus 15:26. "The Lord is the strength of my life" (Psalm 27:1).

- Second-mile leaders know that their work and their times are in God's hands—how they use their time, what motivates their leadership, and where they serve are in the hands of God. They must carefully seek to know how to best use the time that He has granted in their times.

- Second-mile leaders place their families in God's hands. They must commit themselves to being good examples and guardians of the time that they have in the rearing of their children. "And all of thy children shall be taught of the Lord; and great shall be the peace of thy children" (Isaiah 54:13).

- "My times are in thy hands." When these words are believed, received, and depended upon, they bring blessed results in one's life and leadership. "Commit thy way unto the Lord; trust also in Him and He shall bring it to pass" (Psalm 37:5). Committing your ways unto the Lord means recognizing that your times are in His hands.

- Second-mile leaders can enjoy God's peace and actually have hearts that are at rest in the midst of storms, difficulties, trials, and heartaches. Peace is the quietness of the soul in the midst of all these things.

- When we believe, receive, and live by this truth—"my times are in Thy hands"—we (out of necessity) live dependent upon God and receive all of God's blessings.

Scripture: "He has made everything beautiful in its time. He has also set eternity in the hearts of men; yet they cannot fathom what God has done from beginning to end" (Ecclesiastes 3:11, NIV).

Prayer: Lord, my trust is in You as I place my life in Your hands, trusting that You will make everything beautiful in its time. Amen.

The "Time Management" Principle: "So teach us to number our days, that we may apply our hearts unto wisdom" (Psalm 90:12, KJV).

- Second-mile leaders are keenly aware of the brevity of time. One's life span—whether long or short—simply leaves one with many things that they would like to do that they never get done.

- " Realizing that life is short helps us to use the little time we have more wisely and for eternal good. Take time to number your days by asking, "What do I want to see happen in my life before I die? What small step could I take toward that purpose today?"

- "Time is money, and the way we spend it is the principal thing of interest about it." (Accountants' Maxim)[114]

- It has been said that life is like a coin—you can spend it like you want to, but you can only spend it once.

  "He slept beneath the moon,
  He basked beneath the sun;
  He lived a life of going-to-do,
  And died with nothing done."
  (James Albery, 1838–1889)

- "Do nothing in great haste, except catching fleas and running from a mad dog." (Old Farmers' Almanac, 1811)

- Time is:

  "Too Slow for those who Wait,
  Too Swift for those who Fear,
  Too Long for those who Grieve,
  Too Short for those who Rejoice,
  But for those who Love
  Time is not."[115] Henry Van Dyke

Scripture: "Don't waste your time on busy work, mere busy work" (Ephesians 5:16a, *The Message).*

Prayer: Lord, help me to make every minute of every day count—for You and for eternity. Amen.

The "Timing" Principle: "For there is a proper time and procedure for everything" (Ecclesiastes 8:6, NIV).

- Second-mile leaders understand the truth of Ecclesiastes 3:11: "He has made everything beautiful in its time." The timing principle is a matter of critical concern of those who would be leaders.

- The timing principle is content to trust in the providence of God and His timing for our lives in both the good and bad days that may come to us.

- It is possible to be in the wrong place at the wrong time if we step out of God's plan for our lives. "In the spring at the time when kings go off to war, David sent Joab out with the king's men and the whole Israelite army ... but David remained in Jerusalem" (II Samuel 11:1, NIV). When disobedience on our part is evident, we suffer the consequence; yet God has a way of directing us—even through our disobedience.

- "God's timing is always perfect. You see, at just the right time, when we were still powerless, Christ died for the ungodly" (Romans 5:6).

- "God's timing is never too soon nor is it too late. But when the time had fully come, God sent his Son, born of a woman, born under law, to redeem those under law, that we might receive the full rights of sons" (Galatians 4:4–5).

- "Everything in this world has it critical moment; and the height of good conduct consists in knowing and seizing it." (Cardinal de Retz)

- Second-mile leaders seek to synchronize their timing with God's timing for whatever they sense God is leading them to accomplish. They understand the importance of not getting ahead of what God's plans are for their leadership challenges.

- "This time, like all times, is a very good one, if we but know what to do with it." (Ralph Waldo Emerson)

Scripture: "There is a time for everything, and a season for every activity under heaven" (Ecclesiastes 3:1, NIV).

Prayer: Lord, help me to have the proper discernment of the proper time for all the challenges and activities of life. Amen.

The "Times of Life" Principle: "They will bear fruit in old age; they will stay fresh and green, proclaiming, 'The Lord is upright; he is my rock, and there is no wickedness in him' " (Psalm 92:14–15, NIV).

- Second-mile leaders are committed to a lifelong relationship with Christ that will honor Him and allow Him not only to work in them, but also through them for as long as they have life.

- Second-mile leaders have a clear understanding of the times or seasons of life. At every stage of their lives, they are committed to God's plans for them and are perfectly satisfied to be obedient to Him in whatever challenge He places before them.

- Second-mile leaders have developed a personal mission statement that gives them purpose and direction for all the decisions that they are called upon to make. They know what matters most and will not be distracted from their life's mission.

"Whatever is at the center of our life will be the source of our security, guidance, wisdom, and power." (Stephen R. Covey)

- "The secret of life is to have a task, something you devote your entire life to, something you bring everything to, every minute of the day for your whole life." (Henry Moore)

- Second-mile leaders are in full agreement with the Apostle Paul when he says, "But life is worth nothing unless I use it for doing the work assigned to me by the Lord Jesus; the work of telling others the Good News about God's mighty kindness and love" (Acts 20:24, TLB).

- Second-mile leaders know the difference between investing their lives and spending their lives. They invest their lives in those things that have eternal values.

Scripture: "If I live, it will be for Christ, and if I die, I will gain even more" (Philippians 1:21, *The Promise*).

Prayer: Lord, my desire is to serve you faithfully for as long as I have breath. Amen.

The "Rubbish" Principle: "And Judah said, 'The strength of the bearers of burdens is decayed, and there is much rubbish; so that we are not able to build the wall' " (Nehemiah 4:10, KJV).

- Second-mile leaders are constantly reminded that there are many things that hinder their ministry. They have to learn to work around the different things that keep them from focusing on their priorities.

- Dr. E.V Hill's leadership principles are noteworthy. He shared these principles at a conference:

  1. Don't let anyone else raise your babies.
  2. Don't slap a yapping dog.
  3. Learn how to plow around the stumps.

- These timely principles seem to indicate that he gained a lot of experience as how to work around the rubbish that was always there to hinder a leader's progress.

- In the book *The Seven Habits of Highly Effective People,* author Stephen Covey asks this probing question, "Am I able to say no to the unimportant, no matter how urgent, and yes to the important?"

- "A man may be consecrated, dedicated, and devoted, but of little value if undisciplined." (Hudson Taylor)

- "When Henry M. Stanley returned from Africa and his renownd search for David Livingstone, a newsman asked him the facetious question, 'What bothered you the most while you were in Africa, the lions or the snakes?' To which Stanley wryly replied 'Neither! It was the gnats and the mosquitoes!' Our pastors hardly even see the lions and tigers because they are constantly struggling with gnats and mosquitoes."[116]

- Second-mile leaders adopt the old German proverb which states, "The main thing is to keep the main thing the main thing."

- Second-mile leaders are able to keep a singleness of purpose in their hearts as they work and minister by not allowing the rubbish or circumstances of life to hinder their progress.

Scripture: "Therefore, my dear brothers, stand firm. Let nothing move you. Always give yourselves fully to the work of the Lord, because you know that your labor in the Lord is not in vain" (I Corinthians 15:58).

Prayer: Lord, my hope and trust is in You as I live and walk among the rubbish in this world; help me to keep the main thing the main thing. Amen.

The "Success" Principle: "Do not let this Book of the Law depart from your mouth; meditate on it day and night, so that you may be careful to do everything written in it. Then you will be prosperous and successful" (Joshua 1:8, NIV).

- Second-mile leaders know that they may never determine their success based on the secular view of success. True success can only be achieved through their relationship with Christ. Success without a relationship is counterfeit.

- "One's effectiveness in the spirit realm is in direct proportion to his relationship, and his relationship is maintained only by time alone with God and His Word .... The important thing is not the work we may feel we are doing but the relationship we maintain. When relationship is maintained, God's purpose is being accomplished even though visible results may be lacking."[117]

- "Spiritual leaders work from God's agenda. The greatest obstacle to effective spiritual leadership is people pursuing their own plans rather than seeking God's will. God is working throughout the world to achieve His purposes and to advance His kingdom. God's concern is not to advance leaders' dreams and goals or to build their kingdoms. His purpose is to turn His people away from their self-centeredness and their sinful desires and to draw them into a relationship with Him."[118]

- "Satan does not oppose success even in religion if it interferes or prevents relationship, or if it prevents a deep devotional life." (Paul Billheimer)

- Sometimes we forget that our call is to Christ—that our relationship with Christ is the most important aspect of our lives. Our relationship with Christ is more important than the location where we may be attempting to serve Christ. "He called his twelve disciples to him" (Matthew 10:1a, NIV).

- "Measure your faith by your trusting assurance that your Father is too good to forget you, too wise to make a mistake, too loving to let you be ultimately hurt or be the loser, and too mighty ever to be defeated."[119]

Scripture: "For no one can lay any foundation other than the one already laid, which is Christ Jesus. If any man builds on this foundation using gold, silver, costly stones, wood, hay or straw, his work will be shown for what it is, because the day will bring it to light. It will be revealed with fire, and the fire will test the quality of each man's work. If what he has built survives, he will receive his reward. If it is burned up, he will suffer loss; he himself will be saved, but only as one escaping through the flames" (I Corinthians 3:11–15, NIV).

Prayer: Lord, may I always be reminded that success is hearing You say, "Well done." Amen.

The "Rainy Day" Principle: "Within the three days, all the men of Judah and Benjamin had gathered in Jerusalem. And on the twentieth day of the ninth month, all the people were sitting in the square before the house of God, greatly distressed by the occasion and because of the rain" (Ezra 1:9, NIV).

- Ezra certainly was a second-mile leader who had to face some very tough challenges that demanded some very tough leadership decisions. Upon his return to Jerusalem for the rebuilding of the temple, he was confronted with the sinfulness of the people. The forbidden practice of intermarriage with foreign wives was prevalent, which broke his heart. An assembly of all the people had been called to confront the issue and to call for an abandonment of this practice. As they had gathered in Jerusalem for this occasion, they were distressed because of the tough choices that they had to make—but it was also a rainy day.

- Second-mile leaders have to make tough decisions—even on rainy days. Sometimes it is on rainy days that we are forced to take the time to think and pray through the tough leadership decisions that we must make.

- "As for those that think they can lie low until the storm passes, they will be left behind. We can't wait for the storm to blow over; we've got to learn to work in the rain." (Pete Silas, Chairman of Phillips Petroleum)

- "We are either entering a storm, enduring a storm, or emerging from a storm—in which case, we're preparing to enter another storm."Anonymous

- I have heard it said that if you want to see the rainbow, you have to put up with the rain.

- "From the day of your birth till you ride in a hearse, things are never so bad that they couldn't get worse." (Unknown)

- Second-mile leaders are confident that if they are obedient on rainy days, God will bless them—the sun will soon shine on their obedience, and the sunlight will reveal their faithfulness.

Scripture: "Commit your way to the Lord; trust in him and he will do this: He will make your righteousness shine like the dawn, the justice of your cause like the noonday sun" (Psalm 37:5–6, NIV).

Prayer: Lord, my prayer is that I may be able to trust You—even on rainy days. Amen.

Section Eight
The Reward of a Second-Mile Leader

The "God's Faithfulness" Principle: "The one who calls you is faithful and he will do it (I Thessalonians 5:24, NIV).

- Second-mile leaders are dependent upon the faithfulness of the one who has called them and know that He will give the insight, energy, and resourcefulness to do whatever they are asked to do.

- Second-mile leaders have no fear because of God's faithfulness: "So do not fear, for I am with you; do not be dismayed, for I am your God. I will strengthen you and help you; I will uphold you with my right hand" (Isaiah 41:10, NIV).

- Second-mile leaders depend upon God's faithfulness to keep them from the temptations of Satan. "God is faithful, who will not suffer you to be tempted above that ye are able" (I Corinthians 10:13, KJV).

- Second-mile leaders have faith in the one who is faithful for strength and protection as they face the challenges of life and leadership. "But the Lord is faithful, and he will strengthen and protect you from the evil one" (II Thessalonians 3:3, NIV).

- Second-mile leaders live with confidence in the faithfulness of God to do His work in them as well as to do His work through them until they are called home. "Being confident of this, that he who began a good work in you will carry it on to completion until the day of Christ Jesus" (Philippians 1:6, NIV).

- Second-mile leaders are confident that whatever they have committed to God in life and ministry, He is willing to keep and bless in an extraordinary way: "because I know in whom I have believed, and am convinced that he is able to guard what I have entrusted to him for that day" (II Timothy 1:12, NIV).

Scripture: "He will keep you strong to the end, so that you will be blameless on the day of our Lord Jesus Christ. God, who has called you into fellowship with his Son Jesus Christ our Lord, is faithful" (I Corinthians 1:8–9, NIV).

Prayer: My prayer is that You may always remind me of my frailty and Your faithfulness. Amen.

The "Ebenezer" Principle: "Then Samuel took a stone and set it up between Mizpah and Shen. He named it Ebenezer, saying, 'Thus far has the Lord helped us'" (I Samuel 7:12, NIV).

- "Samuel named the newly erected stone monument 'Ebenezer' or 'The Stone of Help' or 'The Help(er) Is a Stone' because the Lord helped [them]. The name given the memorial undoubtedly is a confession of faith and trust in the Lord."[120]

- The Ebenezer stone was a spiritual marker for Israel as to God's deliverance and help in the defeat of their enemies. It was a visible marker to remind them that God had helped them to that point and that He would help them the rest of the way.

- The hymn "Come Thou Fount of Every Blessing" by Robert Robinson takes this event to express:

  "Here I raise mine Ebenezer; hither by thy help I'm come
  And I hope, by thy good pleasure, safely to arrive at home."

- The Ebenezer principle is simply that we must be constantly reminded that God has helped us in the past and that we will rely on His help in the future.

- Second-mile leaders need to take time to look at the Ebenezer stones in their lives—the spiritual markers, the places, and the crossroads where decisions had to be made, directions had to be changed, and maybe even locations have affected their lives in a dramatic way. Dependence on God for help is a normal way for these decisions to be made, because they remember that God has helped them in the past and that He is there for them now.

- Second-mile leaders have learned that they can expect between three and nine turning points or significant changes in their lifetime. When these changes come, it is a great comfort to know that the Ebenezer principle is in effect. God was there before, and God is there now. Looking to Him as the stone of help will always insure victory.

Scripture: "The Lord is my rock, my fortress and my deliverer; my God is my refuge and my Savior" (Psalms 18:2 , NIV).

Prayer: Lord, You are my stone of help in all matters. You are my rock—my solid foundation. Thank You. Amen

The "Cup Running Over" Principle: "You prepare a table before me in the presence of my enemies. You anoint my head with oil; my cup overflows" (Psalm 23:5, NIV).

- Continuous revival is an experience of cups running over or overflowing in the life of a second-mile leader. The joy of the Lord is our strength and our motivation for living.

- Walking with Jesus in the experience of continuous revival gives not only the joy of one's salvation, but also gives freedom to share that joy with those along the way.

- In 1 John 1:3–4, we read, "We proclaim to you what we have seen and heard, so that you also may have fellowship with us. And our fellowship is with the Father and with the Son, Jesus Christ. We write this to make our joy complete." Complete joy is the evidence of cups overflowing.

- "But here comes the point of it in this message of revival. We are to recognize that cups running over is the normal daily experience of the believer walking with Jesus, not the abnormal or occasional, but the normal, continuous experience. But that just isn't so in the lives of practically all of us. Those cups running over get pretty muddled up; other things besides the joy of the Lord flow out of us. We are often much more conscious of emptiness, or dryness, or hardness, or disturbance, or fear, or worry than we are of the fullness of His presence and overflowing joy and peace. And now comes the point. What stops that moment-by-moment flow? The answer is only one, sin."[121]

- Second-mile leaders know that sin of any kind that has come into their lives will stop the flow of the Holy Spirit in His ministry to them and through them. Sin must be removed from their lives, or there will be a loss of the joy of the Lord, and thus the flow of continuous revival will cease.

- "Cups running over" is the Spirit witnessing to Jesus in the heart of the believer. He is our peace, joy, life, all, and it is the Spirit's work never to cease to witness to Him within us. Anything which causes the cups to cease running over is sin." (Norman Grubb)

- "Only one thing separates us from [God]—your iniquities have separated between you and your God, and your sins have hid His face from you. Thank God, the great separation has been replaced by reunion with Him at Calvary, but still the daily incursions of sin in the heart brings about the temporary separation from the sense of His presence; we all know that. The cups do not run over ... for where sin is seen to be sin and confessed as such, the blood is also see to be the blood, praise God, ever cleansing from all unrighteousness; and where the blood cleanses the Spirit always witnesses—and cups run over again."[122]

Scripture: "Do not grieve, for the joy of the Lord is your strength" (Nehemiah 8:10b, NIV).

Prayer: Lord, may my cup always be overflowing and may my leadership come out of that overflow. Amen.

The "Pilgrim" Principle: "These all died in faith, not having received the promises, but having seen them afar off, and were persuaded of them and embraced them, and confessed that they were strangers and pilgrims on the earth" (Hebrews 11:13, KJV).

- Second-mile leaders need to be constantly reminded that they are pilgrims here on earth and are just here for a short time. Their citizenship is in heaven. This being the case, the importance of investing their lives in things that are eternal becomes more pressing.

- The old blue acrylic plaque in my grandmother's house made a lasting impression on my life. Each time that I went to her house for a visit, I would read the following words:

  Only one life
  Twill soon be past
  Only what's done
  For Christ will last

- Second-mile leaders know the difference between spending their lives and investing their lives. Once a life is spent, it is gone. A life invested continues to give rich dividends—not only in a person's lifetime, but in the generations that follow it.

- We are reminded that we have a responsibility to invest our lives in others, so that they may invest their lives in others, in order that they may invest their lives in others, and that they may invest their lives in others … the chain of investment should never be broken. "And the things you have heard me say in the presence of many witnesses entrust to reliable men who will also be qualified to teach others" (II Timothy 2:2, NIV).

- Laying up treasures in heaven becomes a priority of second-mile leaders, because they realize that where their treasures are, their hearts will be as well.

- Second-mile leaders are not conformed or shaped by the values of this world; they are aware that they must be constantly transformed as their minds are renewed by the Holy Spirit.

- Second-mile leaders purposely have set their affections on things above, and not on the things of the earth. They are reminded that "many walk of whom I have told you often … enemies of the cross of Christ … mind earthly things" (Philippians 3:18a, 19b).

Scripture: "By faith he made his home in the promised land like a stranger in a foreign country; he lived in tents, as did Isaac and Jacob, who were his heirs with him of the same promise. For he was looking forward to the city with foundations, whose architect and builder is God" (Hebrews 11:9–10, NIV).

Prayer: Lord, help me to keep my focus on who You are, who I am, where I am, and where I am going. Amen.

The "Blessing" Principle: "God blessed them …. 'Prepare me the kind of tasty food I like and bring it to me to eat, so that I may give you my blessing before I die.' When Esau heard his father's words, he burst out with a loud and bitter cry and said to his father, 'Bless me too, my father'" (Genesis 1:22a, 27:4, 34, NIV).

- Second-mile leaders know the importance of giving their blessing and words of encouragement to others. In their book *The Blessing,* Gary Smalley and John Trent state: "No matter what our age, our parents' approval affects the way we view ourselves—and how we act with those we love most."

- The first mention of blessing is found in Genesis 1:22; the meaning is "bestowal of good." Second-mile leaders know the importance of either giving or withholding words of blessing and encouragement to those they are attempting to lead.

- "Reflect upon your present blessings, of which every man has many; not on your past misfortunes, of which all men have some." (Charles Dickens)

- "He who blesses most is blest." (John Greenleaf Whittier)

- "But words once spoken can never be recalled." (Horace)

- "If thou thinkest twice, before thou speakest once, thou will speak twice better for it." (William Penn)

- "Good words are worth much, and cost little." (George Herbert)

- "I can live for two months on one good compliment." (Mark Twain)

- "I consider my ability to arouse enthusiasm among men the greatest asset I posses. And the way to develop the best that is in a man is by appreciation and encouragement. There is nothing else that so kills the ambitions of men as criticism from their superiors. I never criticize anyone—period. I believe in giving a man an incentive to work. So I am anxious to find praise but loath to find fault." (Charles Schwab)

- Second-mile leaders have determined to be a blessing and to speak words of blessing and encouragement to others. They know the importance of the encouraging words that are spoken and pats on the back to those around them.

Scripture: "Therefore, encourage one another and build each other up, just as in fact you are doing" (I Thessalonians 5:11, NIV).

Prayer: Lord, my prayer is that my life and my lips may always speak words of blessing and encouragement to family and friends. Amen.

The "Being a Blessing" Principle: "And Laban said unto him, 'I pray thee, if I have found favor in thine eyes, tarry: for I have learned by experience that the Lord hath blessed me for thy sake'" (Genesis 30:27, KJV).

- Laban recognized that Jacob's presence had brought the blessings of God upon him and his family. Laban attributed the blessings as being received because of Jacob's relationship with God.

- Second-mile leaders acknowledge that if they are to be a blessing to others, it is because of their relationship to God and their submission to His work in their lives.

- Joseph is recognized as being a blessing to Potiphar's household because of his unyielding confidence in the providence of God to fulfill His purpose for his life. "From the time he put him in charge of his household and all that he owned, the Lord blessed the household of the Egyptian because of Joseph. The blessing of the Lord was on everything Potiphar had both in the house and the field" (Genesis 39:5, NIV).

- Second-mile leaders who have totally committed their lives and leadership to the Lord not only experience God's blessings on their lives, but also see others blessed because of their lives and their leadership.

- Any leadership role brings great responsibility and opportunity to be either a blessing or a hindrance to others. When others are blessed, you as a leader experience an even greater blessing as you see God working in their lives.

- The circumstances surrounding the lives of both Laban and Joseph could have caused them to have become so overcome with their own needs that their lives would not have been a blessing to others. Yet we find that they were able to overcome their own sets of difficulties and allow God to bless others through their lives.

- "I recognize the sublime truth announced in the Holy Scriptures and proven by all history that those nations only are blessed whose God is the Lord." (Abraham Lincoln)

- Second-mile leaders must never become so concerned about their own circumstances that they cannot be a blessing to others. Let others see Jesus in you.

Scripture: "I have learned to be content whatever the circumstances" (Philippians 4:11b, NIV).

Prayer: Lord, my sincere prayer is that my life will always be a genuine blessing to others as Christ is seen in me. Amen.

The "Legacy" Principle: "He died from severe illnesses. But his people did not hold a fire in his honor like his fathers ... Jehoram was thirty-two years old when he became king: he reigned eight years in Jerusalem. He died to no one's regret" (II Chronicles 21:19–20,H CSB).

- Second-mile leaders are aware that they are leaving a legacy that is either positive or negative. It was said of Jehoram that "he died to no one's regret." (II Chronicles 2:20)

- Even though he had served as king of Judah for eight of his forty years of life, Jehoram's life in a place of prominence left no fond memories in the hearts of his followers. There were no memorial flowers or fires to honor his legacy.

- The legacy principle is a reminder that we are all going to leave behind memories that have either been a positive or negative influence on the lives of those we have touched.

- The life and death of Jehoram is a sobering reminder that we should live our lives with focus.

- The second-mile leader lives a life of focus. Our focus should be on leaving a legacy of faithfulness to God. Obedience to God is life's greatest challenge. We must always remember that to obey is better than to sacrifice.

- The second-mile leader leaves a legacy of ministry and service to others. It is understood that Jesus teaches that a great legacy is not achieved through position or power, but rather through servanthood. "You know that the rulers of the Gentiles lord it over them, and their high officials exercise authority over them. Not so with you. Instead, whoever wants to be your servant, and whoever wants to be first must be your slave; just as the Son of Man did not come to be served, but to serve, and give his life as a ransom for many" (Matthew 20:26–28, NIV).

- "He who would be great must be fervent in his prayers, fearless in his principles, firm in his purpose, and faithful in his promises." (Unknown)

- The second-mile leader leaves a legacy that is worth emulating. How do others see you? What kind of life are you reflecting? Will there be those who live out their lives remembering the great spiritual influence that you have left for them to follow?

- Contrast the life of Jehoram, the king, and Dorcas, the seamstress. There were no regrets when the king died. When Dorcas died, the Scriptures say, "And all the widows approached him, weeping and showing him the robes and clothes that Dorcas had made while she was with them" (Acts 9:39). What was the difference? Their lives were lived with a completely different focus. Jehoram was completely inwardly focused, while Dorcas lived a life that was focused outwardly.

Scripture: "If anyone wants to come with me, he must deny himself, take up his cross daily, and follow me" (Luke 9:23, HCSB).

Prayer: Lord, my prayer is that my life may maintain focus on being faithful to You. Amen.

The "Epitaph" Principle: "One day, the evil spirit answered them, 'Jesus I know, and I know about Paul, but who are you?'" (Acts 19:15, NIV).

- Second-mile leaders are keenly aware of the need to live the kind of lives that reflect who they are and what they are trying to accomplish in their place of leadership. They know that they are known not only by their actions but also by their attitudes. How do you want to be known or remembered?

- Stephen R. Covey is widely known for his book and seminar *The Seven Habits of Highly Effective People.* As a part of the seminar, participants are asked to develop a tribute statement that says how they would like to be known or remembered in their relationships with family members and other significant groups of people with whom they have had personal relationships. How do others see you now and how will you be remembered?

- My personal notes reveal what I wrote in 1995 regarding my role as a minister of the gospel as it related to my responsibility as a pastor: "May it be said, he faithfully preached and taught God's Word. He loved us and was a pastor to us in all kinds of situations. He was a godly man."

- What kind of tribute or epitaph are you writing with your life?

  > Your Own Version
  > You are writing a Gospel,
  > A chapter each day,
  > By deeds that you do,
  > By words that you say,
  > Men read what you write,
  > Whether faithless or true;
  > Say, what is the Gospel
  > According to *you?*
  > (Gilbert)[123]

- We are known by our pursuits. My desire is to be known as a man of God. This can only be possible if I determine to pursue Christ with the determination of the apostle Paul as he passionately expresses his heart's desire in Philippians 3:10–11: "I want to know Christ and the power of His resurrection and the fellowship of sharing in His sufferings, becoming like him in death, and so, somehow to attain to the resurrection from the dead."

- Where are you known? Look up your name on an internet search engine such as Google, and it will reveal some of the places that you are known. It will reveal some of the things for which you are known. It will not reveal everything—just some things.

- Is your name written in hell? This is the topic I once heard Leonard Ravenhill address in a message. "One day, the evil spirit answered them, 'Jesus I know, and I know about Paul, but who are you?'" (Acts 19:15) Where do you want your name to be written?

- "Half-heartedness consists of serving God in such a way as not to offend the devil." (Unknown)[124]

- Second-mile leaders need to be reminded of the process of ministry:
  1. Stage One: Desiring to be noticed
  2. Stage Two: Desiring to be remembered
  3. Stage Three: Desiring to make a difference

- One who matures emotionally moves beyond recognition and fame to making a difference in their world.

- Second-mile leaders *make a difference*. Why? Because of the *difference* that Christ has made in their lives.

Scripture: "Well done, good and faithful servant" (Matthew 25:23a).

Prayer: Lord, my prayer is that at the end of the way, I will hear You say, "Well done, good and faithful servant." Amen.

Works Cited

Barna, George. *A Fish Out Of Water.* Nashville: Integrity Publishers, 2002.

—. *Growing True Disciples.* Ventura, CA: Issarchar Resources, 2000.

—. *The Power of Vision.* Ventura, CA: Regal Books, 1992.

—. *The Second Coming of the Church.* Nashville: Word Publishing, 1998.

—. *Turning Vision Into Action.* Ventura, CA: Regal Books, 1996.

Baxter, J. Sidlow. *Does God Still Guide?* Grand Rapids: Zondervan, 1968.

Bedsole, Adolph. *The Pastor in Profile.* Grand Rapids: Baker Book House, 1958.

Bergen, Robert D. *The New American Commentary.* Nashville: Broadman & Holman, 1996.

Billheimer, Paul. *Adventure In Adversity.* Wheaton, Ill: Tyndale House, 1984.

—. *Destined For The Cross.* Wheaton, ILL: Tyndale House, 1982.

—. *Don't Waste Your Sorrows.* Fort Washington, PA: Christian Literature Crusade, 1977.

—. *The Mystery of God's Providence.* Wheaton: Tyndale House, 1984.

Blackaby, Henry and Richard. *Hearing God's Voice*. Nashville: Broadman & Holman, 2002.

Blackaby, Henry and Tom. *The Man God Uses*. Nashville: Broadman & Holman, 1999.

Blackaby, Henry T and Richard. *Spiritual Leadership*. Nashville: Broadman & Holman, 2006.

Blackaby, Henry T. and Brandt, Henry. *The Power of the Call*. Nashville: Broadman & Holman, 1997.

Blanchard, Ken. *Lead Like Jesus*. Nashville: Thomas Nelson, 2003.

Cannon, Jeff and Lt. CMDR. John Cannon. *Leadership Lessons of the Navy SEALS*. New York: McGraw-Hill, 2003.

Chambers, Oswald. *Conformed to His Image*. Fort Washington, PA: Christian Literature Crusade, 1950.

—. *Conformed to His Image*. Fort Washington, PA: Christian Literature Crusade, 1950.

—. *So Send I You*. Fort Washington, PA: Christian Literature Crusade, 1930.

Comfort, Ray. *Hell's Best Kept Secret*. Pittsburg, PA: Whitaker House, 1989.

Cook, Arnold L. *Historical Drift*. Camp Hill, PA: Christian Publications, 2000.

Duewel, Wesley. *Ablaze for God*. Grand Rapids: Francis Asbury Press of Zondervan Publishing House, 1989.

—. *Let God Guide You Daily*. USA: Duwel Literature Trust, Inc., 1988.

—. *Measure Your Life*. Grand Rapids: Zondervan Publishing House, 1992.

—. *Revival Fire*. Grand Radips: Zondervan Publishing House, 1995.

Grubb, Norman. *Continuous Revival*. Washington, Pa.: Christian Literature Crusade, 1971.

Hodges, Herb. *Tallyo-Ho The Fox.* USA: Manhattan Source Inc., 2001.

Haggai, John. *Lead On!* Waco: Word, 1986

J. H., McConkey. *The Surrendered Life.* n.d.

London, H. B. Jr. and Wiseman, Neil B. *The Heart of a Great Pastor.* Ventura, CA: Regal Books, 1994.

Loritts, Crawford. "Qualities of Godly Leadership." *Herald of His Coming* (2009): 1.

Lucado, Max. *On The Anvil.* Wheaton: Tyndale, 1985.

Mansfield, Stephen. *The Faith of George W. Bush.* New York: Penguin Group, 2003.

Maxwell, John. *Failing Forward.* Nashville: Thomas Nelson Publishers, 2000.

Maxwell, L. E. *Crowded To Christ.* Chicago: Moody Press, 1950.

McConkey, J. H. *The Surrendered Life.* n.d.

Paxson, Ruth. *Life on the Highest Plane.* Grand Rapids: Kregel Publications, 1996.

Powell, Paul W. *Getting The Lead Out of Leadership.* Tyler, TX: Dewey Decimal Classification, 1997.

—. *Go-Givers in a Go-Getter World.* Nashville: Broadman, 1986.

Regis, Mike. *Death of the Church.* n.d.

Sanders, Oswald. *Spiritual Leadership.* Chicago: Moody Press, 1967.

—. *Spiritual Lessons.* Chicago: Moody Press, 1944.

Schaller, Lyle. *Getting Things Done.* n.d.

Smith, Hanna Whitall. *The Christian's Secret of a Happy Life.* Old Tappan, NJ: Spire Books, 1966.

Stanley, Charles. *How to Listen to God.* Nashville: Thomas Nelson Publishers, 1985.

Swindoll, Charles. *Starting Over.* Portland: Multnomah, 1977.

Tawes, Roy Lawson. *Lamps in the Darkness.* New York & Nashville: Abingdon-Cokesbury, n.d.

—. *The Global Christ.* New York & Nashville: Abingdon-Cokesbury Press, n.d.

Warren, Rick. *The Purpose Driven Life.* Grand Rapids: Zondervan, 2002.

White, Douglas M. *Holy Ground.* Grand Rapids: Baker Book House, 1962.

End Notes

Section One

1. London, H.B. Jr. and Wiseman, Neil B. *The Heart of a Great Pastor*. Ventura, CA: Regal Books, 1994.

2. London, H.B. Jr. and Wiseman, Neil B. *The Heart of a Great Pastor*. Ventura, CA: Regal Books, 1994.

3. Chambers,Oswald, So Send I You. Fort Washington, Pennsylvania: Christian Literature Crusade,1972

4. London, H.B. Jr. and Wiseman, Neil B. *The Heart of a Great Pastor*. Ventura, CA: Regal Books, 1994.

5. Blackaby, Henry T. and Brandt, Henry. *The Power of the Call*. Nashville: Broadman & Holman, 1997.

6. Blackaby, Henry T. and Brandt, Henry. *The Power of the Call*. Nashville: Broadman & Holman, 1997.

7. Smith, Hanna Whitall. *The Christian's Secret of a Happy Life*. Old Tappan, NJ: Spire Book, 1966.

8. Stanley, Charles. *How to Listen to God*. Nashville: Thomas Nelson Publishers, 1985.

9. Smith, Hanna Whitall. *The Christian's Secret of a Happy Life*. Old Tappan, NJ: Spire Book, 1966.

10. Smith, Hanna Whitall. *The Christian's Secret of a Happy Life.* Old Tappan, NJ; Spire Books, 1966.

11. Duewel, Wesley. *How to Measure Your Life.* Grand Rapids: Zondervan Publishing House, 1992.

12. Blackaby, Henry and Richard. *Hearing God's Voice.* Nashville: Broadman & Holman, 2002.

13. Duewel, Wesley. *Let God Guide You Daily* USA: Duewel Literature Trust, Inc.,1988.

14. Sanders, Oswald. *Spiritual Lessons.* Chicago: Moody Press, 1944.

15. Baxter, J. Sidlow. *Does God Still Guide?* Grand Rapids: Zondervan, 1968.

16. Sanders, Oswald. *Spiritual Lessons.* Chicago: Moody Press, 1944.

17. Loritts, Crawford. *Herald of His Coming,* Feburary 2009.

18. DeMoss, Nancy Leigh. *Herald of His Coming,* Feburary 2009.

19. Loritts, Crawford. Herald of His Coming, February 2009

20. Loritts, Crawford. *Herald of His Coming,* Feburary 2009.

21. Sanders, J. Oswald. *Spiritual Leadership.* Chicago: Moody Press, 1967.

22. Duewel, Wesley. *Ablaze For God.* Grand Rapids: Zondervan Publishing House, 1989.

23. Brown , Mary. I'll Go Where You Want Me To Go. Word/ Integrity Music. USA,1997

Section Two

24. Duewel, Wesley. *Ablaze For God.* Grand Rapids: Zondervan Publishing House, 1989.

25. Blackaby, Henry and Tom. *The Man God Uses.* Nashville: Broadman & Holman 1999.

26. Sanders, J. Oswald. *Spiritual Leadership.* Chicago: Moody Press, 1967.

27. Sanders, J. Oswald. Spiritual Leadership. Chicago: Moody Press, 1977

28. Duewel, Wesley. Measure Your Life. Grand Rapids: Zondervan Publishing House, 1992

29. Billheimer, Paul. *Adventures in Adversity.* Wheaton: Tyndale House, 1984.

30. Billheimer, Paul. *Adventures in Adversity.* Wheaton: Tyndale House, 1984.

31. Billheimer, Paul. Destined for the Cross. Wheaton: Tyndale House, 1982

32. Billheimer, Paul. Don't Waste Your Sorrows. Fort Washington, PA: Christian Literature Crusade, 1977

33. Billheimer, Paul. *Don't Waste Your Sorrows.* Fort Washington, PA: Christian Literature Crusade,1977.

34. Billheimer, Paul. *Adventures in Adversity.* Wheaton: Tyndale House,1984.

35. Billheimer, Paul. *Adventures in Adversity.* Wheaton: Tyndale House,1984.

36. L.R., Scarborough With Christ After The Lost. Nashville: Broadman Press, 1952

37. Hodges, Herb. Tallyo-Ho The Fox. USA: Manhattan Source Inc. 2001

38. Billheimer, Paul. *Destined for the Cross.* Wheaton: Tyndale House, 1982.

39. Criswell, W.A. & Patterson, Paige. Heaven. Wheaton: Tyndale House,1991

40. Chambers, Oswald. My Utmost for His Highest. Uhrichsville, OH: Barbour and Company,Inc.1963

41. Sanders, J. Oswald. Spiritual Leadership. Chicago: Moody Press,1977

42. Oatman, Jr. Johnson. The Celabration Hymnal,U.S.A: Word Music/Integrity Music, 1997

Section Three

43. Paxson, Ruth. *Life on the Highest Plane*. Grand Rapids: Kregel Publications, 1996.

44. Paxson, Ruth. *Life on the Highest Plane*. Grand Rapids: Kregel Publications, 1996.

45. Cook, Arnold. *Historical Drift*. Camp Hill, PA: Christian Publications, 2000.

46. Bounds, E.M . Power Through Prayer. Grand Ripids: Zondervan, 1972

47. Maxwell, L.E. Crowded to Christ. Chicago: Moody Press, 1976

48. Mansfield, Stephen. *The Faith of George W. Bush*. New York: Penguin Group, 2003.

49. Powell, Paul. *Getting the Lead Out of Leadership*. USA: 1997.

50. Sanders, J. Oswald. *Spiritual Leadership*. Chicago: Moody Press, 1967.

51. Sanders, J. Oswald. *Spiritual Leadership*. Chicago: Moody Press, 1967.

52. Cook, Arnold. *Historical Drift*. Camp Hill. PA: Christian Publications, 2000.

53. Cook, Arnold. Historical Drift: Camp Hill,PA: Christian Publications, 2000

54. Cook, Arnold. *Historical Drift:* Camp Hill, PA: Christian Publications, 2000.

55. Comfort, Ray. *Hell's Best Kept Secret.* Pittsburg: Whitaker House, 1989 .

56. Cannon, Jeff and Lt.Cmdr. John Cannon. *Leadership Lessons of the Navy Seals.* New York: McGraw-Hill, 2003.

57. Billheimer, Paul. *The Mystery of God's Providence.* Wheaton: Tyndale House,1984.

58. Blackaby, Henry and Richard. *Spiritual Leadership.* Nashville: Broadman & Holman, 2006.

59. De Jong, Benjaman R. Uncle Ben's Quotebook. Irvine California: Harvest House Publishers,1978

60. Mead, Frank S. Encylopedia of Religious Quotations. London: Peter Davies. Nd

61. Mead, Frank S. Encylopedia of Religious Quotations, London: Peter Davies. Nd

62. Mead, Frank S. Encylopedia of Religious Quotations. London: Peter Davies. Nd

63. De Jong, Benjaman R. Uncle Ben's Quotebook. Irvine California: Harvest House Publishers, 1978

64. Duewel, Wesley L. Measure Your Life. Grand Rapids: Zondervan,1991

65. Blanchard, Ken. *Lead Like Jesus.* Nashville: Thomas Nelson, 2003.

66. Haggai, John. *Lead On!* Waco: Word, 1986.

Section Four

67. Foster, Richard J. Celebration of Discipline. SanFranciso : HarperCollins Publishers, 1988

68. Blanchard, Ken. *Lead Like Jesus.* Nashville: Thomas Nelson, 2003.

69. Blanchard, Ken. *Lead Like Jesus.* Nashville: Thomas Nelson, 2003.

70. Cook, Arnold. *Historical Drift.* Camp Hill, PA: Christian Publications, 2000.

71. Cook, Arnold. *Historical Drift.* Camp Hill, PA: Christian Publications, 2000.

72. Duewel, Wesley. *Revival Fire.* Grand Rapids: Zondervan,1995.

73. Duewel, Wesley. *Revival Fire.* Grand Rapids: Zondervan,1995.

74. Eigen, Lewis D. & Siegel, Jonathan P. The Manager's Book of Quotations. Rockville; AMACOM, 1991

Section Five

75. Barna, George. *A Fish Out of Water.* Nashville: Integrity Publishers, 2002.

76. Barna, George. *A Fish Out of Water.* Nashville: Integrity Publishers, 2002.

77. Duewel, Wesley. *How to Measure Your Life.* Grand Rapids: Zondervan, 1992.

78. Duewel, Wesley. *How to Measure Your Life.* Grand Rapids: Zondervan, 1992.

79. Blanchard, Ken. Lead Like Jesus. Nashville: Thomas Nelson, 2003

80. Sanders, J. Oswald. *Spiritual Leadership.* Chicago: Moody Press, 1967.

81. De Jong, Benjamin R. *Uncle Ben's Quote Book.* Irvine: 1976.

82. Sanders, J. Oswald. *Spiritual Leadership.* Chicago: Moody Press, 1967.

83. Barna, George. *A Fish Out of Water*. Nashville: Integrity Publishers, 2002.

84. Duewel, Wesley. *Ablaze For God*. Grand Rapids: Zondervan Publishing House, 1989.

85. Bedsole, Adolph. The Pastor in Profile. Grand Rapids: Baker Book House, 1958

86. Thomas, Major W. Ian. *The Saving Life of Christ*. Grand Rapids: Zondervan, 1961.

87. Maxwell, L.E. *Crowded to Christ*. Chicago: Moody Press, 1950.

88. Maxwell, L.E. *Crowded to Christ*. Chicago: Moody Press, 1950.

89. Eigen, Lewis D. & Siegel, Jonathan P. The Manager's Book of Quotations. Rockville: AMACOM,1991

90. Maxwell, L.E. *Crowded to Christ*. Chicago: Moody Press, 1950.

91. Chambers, Oswald. *So Send I You:* Fort Washington, PA: Christian Literature Crusade 1950.

92. Hodges, Herb. *Tallyo-Ho The Fox*. USA: Manhattan Source Inc., 2001.

93. Sanders, J. Oswald. *Spiritual Leadership*. Chicago: Moody Press, 1967.

94. Billheimer, Paul. *The Mystery of God's Providence*. Wheaton: Tyndale House,1984.

95. Blackaby, Henry and Richard. *Spiritual Leadership*. Nashville: Broadman & Holman, 2006.

Section Six

96. De Jong, Benjamin R.Uncle Ben's Quotebook.Irvine, California: Harvest House Publishers, 1976

97. De Jong, Bengamin R. Uncle Ben's Quotebook. Irvine, California: Harvest House Publishers,1976.

98. London, H.B. Jr. and Wiseman, Neil B. *The Heart of a Great Pastor.* Ventura, CA: Regal Books,1994.

99. Paxson, Ruth. *Life on the Highest Plane.* Grand Rapids: Kregel Publications, 1996.

100. Paxson, Ruth. *Life on the Highest Plane.* Grand Rapids: Kregel Publications,1996.

101. Duewel, Wesley. *Ablaze For Go.,* Grand Rapids: Zondervan Publishing House, 1989.

102. White, Douglas M. *Holy Ground.* Grand Rapids: Baker Book House,1962.

103. Swindoll, Charles. *Starting Over.* Portland: Multnomah Press,1977.

104. Paxson, Ruth. *Life on the Highest Plane.* Grand Rapids: Kregel Publications, 1996.

105. McConkey, J.H. *The Surrendered Life.*

106. Tawes, Roy Lawson. *Lamps in the Darkness.* New York & Nashville: Abingdon-Cokesbury, n.d

107. Tawes, Roy Lawson. *Lamps in the Darkness.* New York & Nashville: Abingdon- Cokesbury, n.d

Section Seven

108. Tawes, Roy Lawson. The Global Christ. New York & Nashville: Abingdon-Cokesbury Press, n.d.

109. Chambers, Oswald. *Conformed to His Image.* Fort Washington, PA: Christian Literature Crusade, 1950.

110. Chambers, Oswald. *Conformed to His Image.* Fort Washington, PA: Christian Literature Crusade, 1950.

111. Chambers, Oswald. *Conformed to His Image.* Fort Washington, PA: Christian Literature Crusade, 1950.

112. Maxwell, John. *Failing Forward.* Nashville: Thomas Nelson Publishers, 2000.

113. Sanders, J. Oswald. *Spiritual Leadership.* Chicago: Moody Press, 1967.

114. Eigen, Lewis D. % Seigel, Jonathan P. The Manager's Book of Quotations. Rockville: AMACOM, 1991

115. Eigen, Lewis D. & Seigel, Jonathan P. The Manager's Book of Quotations. Rockville: AMACOM, 1991

116. Hodges, Herb. *Tallyo-Ho The Fox.* USA: Manhattan Source Inc., 2001.

117. Billheimer, Paul. *The Mystery of God's Providence.* Wheaton: Tyndale House,1984.

118. Blackaby, Henry and Richard. *Spiritual Leadership.* Nashville: Broadman & Holman, 2006.

119. Duewel, Wesley. *How to Measure Your Life.* Grand Rapids: Zondervan ,1992.

Section Eight

120. Bergen, Robert D. *The New American Commentary.* Nashville: Broadman & Holman, 1996.

121. Grubb, Norman. *Continuous Revival,* Washington, PA: Christian Literature Crusade, 1971.

122. Grubb, Norman. Continuous Revival. Washington Pa: Chrisitian Literature Crusade, 1971.

123. De Jong, Benjamin R. Uncle Ben's Quotebook,Irvine, California: Harvest House,1976.

124. De Jong, Benjamin R. Uncle Ben's Quotebook, Irvine California: Harvest House, 1976